SEWING BASICS

SEWING BASICS

CREATING A STYLISH WARDROBE
WITH STEP-BY-STEP TECHNIQUES

PATRICIA MOYES

The Taunton Press

Publisher: Jim Childs

Acquisitions Editor: Jolynn Gower

Editorial Assistant: Sarah Coe

Copy Editor: Gilda Caserta

Layout Artist: Suzie Yannes

Photographers: Jack Deutsch, Susan Kahn

Illustrator: Kathy Bray

Indexer: Lynda Stannard

Taunton
BOOKS & VIDEOS
for fellow enthusiasts

Printed in the United States of America

10 9 8 7 6 5 4 3 2 1

The Taunton Press, Inc., 63 South Main Street,

PO Box 5506, Newtown, CT 06470-5506

e-mail: tp@taunton.com

Distributed by Publishers Group West

Library of Congress Cataloging-in-Publication Data

Moyes, Pat.
    Sewing basics : creating a stylish wardrobe with step-by-step techniques / Patricia Moyes.
        p.   cm.
    ISBN 1-56158-266-2
        1. Machine sewing. 2. Tailoring (Women's). I. Title.
    TT713.M69   1999
    646.2'044—dc21   98–55587
                                                              CIP

To my students: Annette, Lori, Heather, Rubi, Susan, Kimberley, Marcia, Lynn, Leslie, David, Doris, Renee, and Betty. By teaching them, I have learned what's important to teach.

acknowledgments

My sewing classes at The Sewing Workshop in San Francisco are here between the pages of Sewing Basics. So important a project cannot be produced without help, and I was fortunate to have lots of it. If stars were to be awarded for help, they would go to Jolynn for pitching me this project; to Sarah for keeping me on track and helping along the way; to Susan for her incredible talent; to Mom and Dad for their support; and to Jennifer and David for advice, encouragement, friendship, and Sunday brunches.

contents

introduction

I was very little when I began to sew. I learned to make doll clothes from my beloved Great Aunt Julie, probably when I was about three or four. I got to pick up pins with a magnet in her sewing room, but I did learn how to sew fabric pieces right sides together, how to gather a skirt, and how to sew on a snap. My dolls were very well dressed, thanks to Aunt Julie.

In my family, all of us were well dressed. Aunt Julie created doll clothes and Easter dresses, dance costumes and wedding outfits. Most of our clothes were bought, but inspired by Aunt Julie, we assembled and coordinated our outfits with much thought given to what each person should wear. Because of Aunt Julie, I have always associated sewing with the creation of clothes.

By the time I was a teenager, my interest was no longer "clothes." It was "fashion." My new idol was my big sister who was on the teen board of one of San Francisco's big department stores. She had a flair for putting outfits together, a flair for fashion. We poured over the fashion magazines, especially the fall issues, a habit I admit to still having. We decided what we liked and what we needed, and we cut out pictures and planned our wardrobes. Since I had learned to sew on the sewing machine, I made a lot of my wardrobe pieces.

Learning to sew was never a dreadful experience for me. Instead, my memories are of the special things I made, the sewing techniques I learned along the way, the little tricks that many women who sewed passed on to me during those years. I remember the grey wool dress I made for my mom, a Vogue pattern with four bound buttonholes and a gusset in each sleeve—very Jackie Kennedy. I remember the silk linen dress I made from fabric that cost a then-outrageous $8 per yard. I remember the little kit I had for making the bound buttonholes; the instructions were so well written and funny, too. I remember learning about interfacing in college from a friend's mom, who is still one of my few sewing friends. I remember making quilted jackets for extra money, which allowed me to perfect binding edges. I remember the lady down the street who taught me to understitch facings, which really made my clothes look good.

Yes, I had a knack, but I had help along the way.

Sewing Basics is about help along the way. It is about beginning to sew clothes. It's not an encyclopedia, because it's not about everything, but it has all the tricks and tips that I can think of that work when making easy garments. This book has the information you need to read between the lines in the pattern instructions, so that even when you are beginning to sew, you can make easy clothes that look good, that you like, and that you will want to wear.

before you sew

■ ■ 1 ■

So, you want to sew.

I can't remember a time when I didn't want to sew, and even now I'm always trying to find more time for it.

I'm not sure whether it's the clothes I'm interested in making or if it's that I like combining pattern with fabric and even combining color and texture and drape of fabric. I do know I like having the right materials on hand if I suddenly find myself with time to sew.

This chapter is an introduction to the things you need to know to get started. Fabrics, tools, patterns, even your sewing machine should be a little less mysterious after reading this.

Mock wrap skirt
Pattern: Burda 3343 (discontinued)
Fabric: Wool jersey
Needle: 80/12 H
Thread: Mettler silk finish cotton
Straight stitch, 0.5 zigzag, 2.5

Raglan T-shirt
Pattern: Burda 3065
Fabric: Cotton knit
Needle: 80/12 H
Thread: Dual Duty polyester
Straight stitch, 0.5 zigzag, 2.5

■ FABRIC

Fabric is wonderful. It comes in a gazillion colors and prints. Fabric drapes, it flows, it's soft or silky or velvety or… I could go on but you get the idea. But if you are beginning to sew, you might not know that some fabrics are easier to work with than others. A few fabrics are less wonderful because they are difficult to cut, handle, sew, and press. Some basic information can help.

Types of fabrics

Fabric is either knit or woven (see the photo below). If you have ever knit or crocheted, you know that yarn is looped in the process of making a stitch. The same is true for knit fabric. It is the looping of the yarn that allows the garment to stretch. T-shirts and swimsuits are examples of garments constructed with fabrics

that are knit. The stretch in knit fabrics makes them especially suitable for actionwear in particular and sportswear in general. Sewing with knit fabric requires you to consider the stretch before you choose the garment style. You will have to choose a sewing-machine stitch that accommodates the stretch, too, and maybe even change the needle type and size.

Woven fabric is fabric that is constructed with two sets of yarn that are perpendicular to each other: the warp and the weft. If you have ever seen a weaver work, you will recall that there is a loom with fixed threads (the warp) and a shuttle that weaves the horizontal (weft or woof) thread to create the fabric. This fabric is stable and not meant to stretch. Woven fabric can have interesting surface textures, like velvet, silk, and damask. Wovens dominate the fabric used by home sewers. The variety of woven fabric available is vast. There are light-weight, sheer, and delicate wovens, as well as dense, heavy wovens.

Beyond the choices of knit or woven, there is another aspect to consider: Is the fabric a natural fiber or a man-made fiber? Natural fibers include cotton, linen, wool, and silk. Rayon, which is made from wood pulp, can be considered a natural fiber, too. Acrylic, polyester, nylon, lycra, polyfleece, spandex, and triacetate are man-made. Microfibers, which often include natural-fiber components, frequently have to be handled in the same manner as man-made fibers.

The easiest fabrics to work with are the ones that are made of natural fibers, some knit and some woven. My easy-fabric list includes cot-

Fabric is either knit or woven. The knit fabric on the left is a cotton-and-spandex blend, and the woven fabric on the right is linen.

Natural fibers, which include cotton, cotton knit, linen, cotton and linen blends, wool jersey, wool crepe, and rayon, are the easiest fabrics to work with.

ton, cotton knit, cotton flannel, silk noil, lightweight wool and wool crepe, wool jersey and double-knit, most rayons except sueded rayons and very drapey ones, and light- to middleweight linen (see the photo above). Linen blended with rayon or cotton is all right, but avoid linen blended with polyester. Fleece is on the list, too, as well as man-made stretchy fabrics such as velour and spandex blended with wool or cotton but not with acrylic or polyester.

> **tip** *Look for fabric that is not too stiff or bulky and that drapes well. This is a general rule for clothing construction. Bulky fabrics make the body look…well, bulky. You won't like the way you look in garments made with these fabrics.*

It is important to avoid fabric that requires extra handling when you are learning to sew. Some wools like gabardine require extra attention to detail when pressing; silks and slinky fabrics are more difficult to cut and handle while sewing; and polyester fabrics, while easy to care for, are not always easy to manipulate.

When you are new to sewing, stay with the list of easy fabrics. Until you gain confidence about your sewing skills, let yourself be challenged by the garment style, not by the fabric.

Preparing the fabric

Once you have chosen a fabric for your project, it is necessary to prepare it for sewing. For the most part, this means to wash it or steam it with an iron, depending on whether or not it is washable. Then you need to press out any wrinkles.

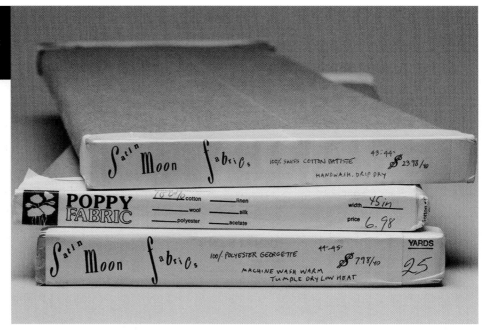

Look on the end of a fabric bolt for fabric content as well as care instructions.

But even this simple instruction invokes a few questions: How do you know if the fabric is washable? Will it shrink? How much? Here are some easy answers: When you buy fabric, look at the end of the bolt for washing instructions, or ask the salesperson if the fabric is washable and if it shrinks (see the photo above).

COTTON Cotton is a washable fabric that sometimes shrinks and sometimes doesn't. To be on the safe side, whenever the fabric is cotton, a cotton blend, or even a cotton knit, buy a bit more to allow for shrinkage. Wash it in the washing machine and dry it in the dryer, using the temperatures you would use for the finished garment you are going to make.

LINEN With a few exceptions, wash linen in the washing machine and dry it in the dryer before sewing. Don't wash black linen because it will

tip *To prepare a fabric by steaming it, press it with an iron set on the steam setting and in the temperature range for your fabric. Press the entire piece of fabric two or three times, shooting lots of steam into the fabric as you go. Watch out for drips, which can mar some fabrics like rayon, and for steam marks that result from using too high a temperature setting. You can get a bit more steam if you hold the iron about ½ in. above the surface of the fabric, but it will take you longer to prepare it this way. This is, however, a great way to steam wool.*

get grayer, and don't mix bright colors with other laundry, since the dye may bleed out.

RAYON Some rayons are washable and some are not. Pay attention to the instructions at the end of the bolt. If the fabric is not washable, steam the entire length of the fabric.

WOOL Wool also needs to be steamed, which you can do at home or you can bring the fabric to your dry cleaner and ask if they will do it for you. You don't need to dry-clean the fabric unless it is white. White wool tends to shrink even after the garment is made because neither the fibers nor the fabric have been exposed to the heat that they would have had they been dyed.

WHEN YOU ARE NOT SURE If you are in doubt whether to prewash the fabric or not, purchase an extra ⅛ yd., cut it off, and measure it for length and width. Wash it in the washing machine and dry it in the dryer, press it, then measure it again. Is it still 4½ in. long and as wide as the piece you bought? Did it fade or did the bright color bleed into the lighter part of the print? Is the surface duller than the unwashed piece or is the surface scuffed in any way? If you like the results, wash the rest of the fabric with the peace of mind that you won't ruin your investment. If you don't like the results, prepare the fabric by steaming it, then dry-clean the finished garment (see the photo below).

Fabric characteristics

Once you have prepared the fabric for sewing, it's time to take a closer look at it.

SELVAGES Fabric has selvage edges. These are the hard or stiff edges of the fabric that define the fabric's width. Sometimes there are little holes where the fabric was attached to the

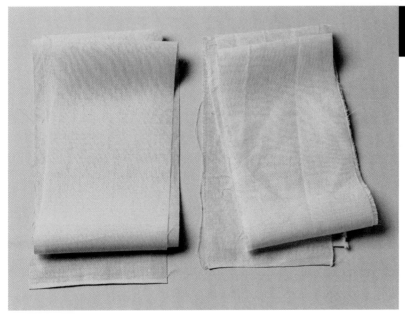

When you are not sure if a fabric is washable, test-wash ⅛ yd. to see if it shrinks, ravels, or fades.

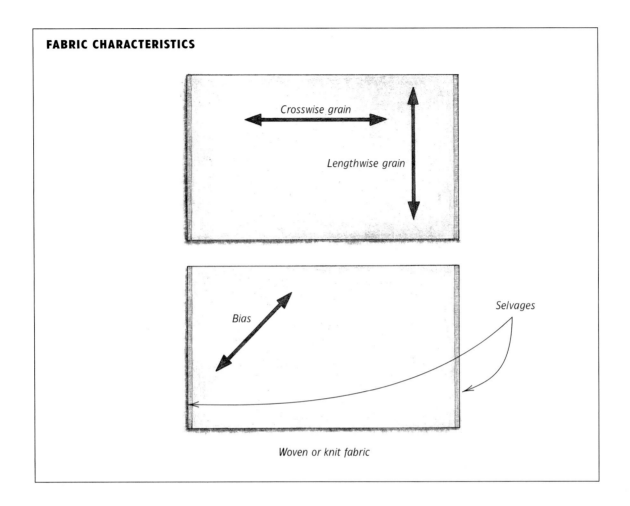

FABRIC CHARACTERISTICS

Crosswise grain

Lengthwise grain

Bias

Selvages

Woven or knit fabric

loom and sometimes there is a woven or print-ed logo along the selvage edges (see the bot-tom illustration above).

GRAIN Fabric has directional grain. The length-wise grain is parallel to the selvage edge, while the crosswise grain runs from selvage edge to selvage edge (see the top illustration above). In a knit fabric, both the lengthwise grain and the crosswise grain stretch, although the crosswise grain is stretchier. In a woven fabric, both the lengthwise grain and the crosswise grain are stable, but there may be some give in the cross-wise grain.

Between the two grainlines is the bias, which is not a grain but a direction. Even in a woven fabric the bias is stretchy, which is good when we want to use the stretch and not so good if we don't. In a knit fabric, the lengthwise grain and the crosswise grain are both stretchy, but the lengthwise grain tends to be less so. Bias is used less often in knits.

NAP Fabric can have nap, which is a raised surface that is sometimes textured. Think of corduroy or velvet. Run your hand over the fabric along the lengthwise grain, parallel to the selvages, moving one way, then the other.

Note that there is a smoother direction, much like there is a smoother direction when you pet a cat. On a garment, it is desirable to have the smooth direction run from the bottom to the top. All of the "up" ends of the pattern pieces (the neck edges, the top of the sleeves, the waist edge) need to be positioned on the fabric the same way so that the smoothness of the nap runs from the bottom of the piece to the top. The fabric will look richer and, when you sit, the nap won't be crushed.

PRINTS Fabric prints are sometimes directional (see the illustrations on p. 10). Imagine a fabric with flowers on stems. The flowers might be scattered on the fabric, some up and some down; there is no correct up or down on this fabric. But the flowers might have their blossoms in the same direction, making this a directional print. Just as with a napped fabric, you need to place all of the top edges of the pattern pieces in the same way so that the print is going in the right direction on every piece—you don't want the flowers upside down on one side and sideways on the sleeve.

Border prints are examples of fabrics that are directional on the crossgrain. Stripes that run from selvage to selvage are directional, too. With these fabrics, pattern pieces need to be laid out on the crossgrain, with the tops of the pattern pieces facing up along one of the selvage edges.

Some directional prints or stripes run diagonally on the fabric. Simple garments can often accommodate these and, in fact, look terrific. Look for fabric suggestions on the back of the pattern envelope, though. "Not suitable for diagonal prints" may be the pattern company's advice for some styles.

Additional yardage is often needed when you are working with napped fabric, directional

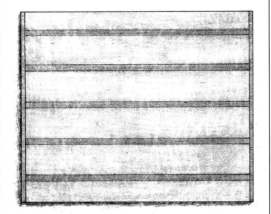

Striped fabric can be directional.

Directional prints

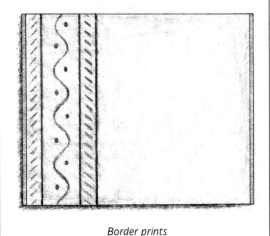

Border prints

prints, and striped (or plaid) fabric. The back of the pattern envelope is the place to check for information about what kind and how much fabric you need for your project. If you are looking for an easy project, however, you might want to avoid the hassle of working with these types of fabric.

■ BASIC SEWING TOOLS

Before you begin to sew, you need to assemble a few good sewing tools. Let's review the basic tool kit.

Scissors

Everyone who sews needs to have a good pair of sharp scissors for cutting fabric. Choose a pair that is right-handed or left-handed (whichever you are) that you will keep with your sewing supplies, not used for cutting coupons and wrapping paper.

Scissors range from the small embroidery type to large dressmaker shears. For starters, find a pair of scissors 8 in. to 10 in. long; your second pair can be small scissors for trimming and clipping.

Pinking shears

Pinking shears are a handy tool for simple seam finishing. These large scissors cut a wavy or V-shaped edge. They should not be used for cutting out pattern pieces though, because the cut edge is not exact and cutting should be as exact as possible.

Every sewer needs a tool kit with cutting, measuring, and marking devices, sharp pins, needles, and a seam ripper.

Pins

Buy sharp pins and throw away any pin that is bent, dull, or burred. Sharp pins work in both fine and heavy fabrics. Good pins are available with small and large glass heads and with no heads at all. I find pins with glass heads are a good choice because they can be seen in the fabric (and on the floor, too). Beware of pins with plastic heads because the heads melt if pressed with a hot iron.

It is a good idea to have a place to keep your pins. I know sewers who like to keep their pins in boxes and sewers who prefer to stick their pins into pincushions. I like a magnetic pin-cushion and only buy pins that will stick. Then when I knock the pincushion over and spill all the pins, I just sweep the floor with the pin-cushion to easily collect them.

Needles

You will need to have an assortment of needles for hand sewing and needles for your sewing machine in your sewing tool kit.

HAND-SEWING NEEDLES Needles for hand sewing come in various lengths, numbered sizes, eye sizes, and fineness, and with names such as betweens, sharps, embroidery/crewels (not to be confused with needles for tapestry-type

> **tip** *A needle should be sharp enough to easily pierce the fabric, but it shouldn't be too thick or else it will mar the fabric. The thread you are using should fit through the eye of the needle; if not, choose a needle with a larger eye. If you have trouble threading a needle, look for a Calyx-eye needle that has a fine but large eye at the top.*

crewel embroidery), darners, and beadings. Needle sizes range from 1 to 24; the smaller the number is, the longer and thicker it is. Keep a variety of hand-sewing needles in your sewing kit for marking, basting, hemming, and sewing on snaps and buttons.

SEWING-MACHINE NEEDLES Sewing-machine needles also should be chosen for the type and weight of fabric you are using. Machine needles are numbered by size and lettered to indicate the shape of the tip—both are important. The sizes are a pair of numbers: the European number and the American number. 60/8 is a fine needle, suitable for use with very lightweight or fine fabrics like chiffon. 70/10 and 80/12 are the frequently used sizes for light-to-medium and medium-weight fabrics. 90/14 is used for fabrics like corduroy, and 100/16 is for even heavier fabrics like upholstery fabric.

Needle type is as important as size. Choose an H needle for most general sewing, whether the fabric is woven or knit. Choose an SUK needle for use with power knits or fabrics that are blended with spandex and an H-S needle for knit fabrics where the H needle leaves skipped stitches. H-J needles are for jeans, and NTW needles are for real leather, because they punch holes in the fabric.

N needles are designed for topstitching because they have large eyes to accommodate the width of heavier topstitching thread.

Microtex Sharp Needles are now available for use with microfibers. Some sewers find that small jeans (70/10 H-J) needles also work with this fabric.

Another kind of needle is the double needle, which can be used with woven fabrics as well as knits. These needles create very ready-to-wear finishes, especially on knits.

Gayle Grigg Hazen, a popular and knowledgeable sewing teacher in the San Jose, California, area, is, among other things, the teaching guru regarding sewing machines and needles. She gives the best advice: Change the sewing-machine needle often. Don't let the needle be the source of any sewing problem.

> **tip** *Use the appropriate needle for your project, then throw it away before you start another. If you are working with a microfiber, you may have to change the needle several times during the course of the project.*

There are three easy ways to use a seam ripper and one way you should never use one.

For the first method, you need only remove the stitches from the area where the mistake is. There is no reason to take out a whole seam if only 2 in. need to be fixed. Using the sharp point of the seam ripper, isolate the thread from the fabric. Slide the cutting edge toward the thread to cut it. Use the long point to pull out each of the stitches you need to remove (see the photo below).

The second method you might try, perhaps if you are removing thread from a long section, is to cut the thread at the beginning of the stitches to be removed and use the point of the seam ripper to pull out a number of threads so that you end up with a tail. Move along the row for about an inch and cut the thread, then use the thread tail to pull out this inch of stitches. Flip to the opposite side of the seam, where there is now a 1-in. tail, and repeat (see the photo at right).

A third, fast way of removing stitches with a seam ripper is to cut every third or fourth stitch along the seam you are removing. On the opposite side, pull the thread. All of the stitches should come out, although you may need to tug a bit, and then you will need to remove all the little cut threads.

Sometimes it is necessary to pull the seamed pieces apart and rip out the stitches between them. This happens when it is hard to isolate the thread from the fabric because the color match is so good (like black thread in black fabric) or when the thread has blended itself into the fabric because the weave is knubby or loose. Pulling the pieces apart pulls the first couple of stitch-es apart. Carefully isolate the thread with the tip of your seam ripper, and cut one or two stitches at a time until you have removed all the stitches you need to take out. Here's where you should *not* line up the seam ripper and just cut between the fabric pieces— resist the temptation! This is a very good way of cutting the fabric and not just the thread, creating a bigger disaster than a seam that needs to be resewn.

Pull the thread out on one side, which will leave you a tail to pull on the other.

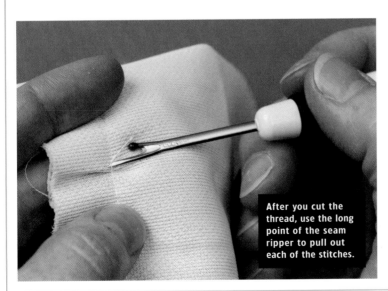

After you cut the thread, use the long point of the seam ripper to pull out each of the stitches.

Tape measures

No sewing kit would be complete without a tape measure. Tape measures are available in several widths, from ½ in. to 1 in. If you have to choose one, ⅝ in. is a good width.

Seam rippers

One of the best things about sewing is that you can remove and redo your mistakes. This tool can help. Seam rippers have an uneven, forked end with a cutting edge between the fork tips. Look for a seam ripper whose fork tips are sharp and not too thick so that you can work with fine fabrics as well as medium-to-heavy ones. (See "How to Use a Seam Ripper" on p. 13.)

Tracing paper, chalk, and other marking devices

I am a classicist who makes tailor tacks to transfer certain markings from the pattern to the fabric. However, I keep tracing paper and a tracing wheel in my sewing kit, as well as chalk of various types and marking pens, and I use all of them at different times.

Tracing paper is paper that is waxed on one side. Tracing-paper packages contain sheets of various colors, usually white, red, blue, and yellow. When a tracing wheel is rolled over the wrong side of the paper, the colored wax is transferred to the fabric underneath.

The chalk marker I use most frequently is the Chalkoner. I can draw fine lines for such tasks as buttonholes with this device. I also like chalk pencils for quick marking. In addition, there are marking pens and pencils available, some that brush off and some that disappear with

THREAD USAGE FOR VARIOUS FABRICS	
FABRIC	**THREAD**
Cotton	Cotton thread
Cotton knit	Cotton or polyester thread
Cotton flannel	Cotton thread
Silk noil	Cotton or polyester thread
Lightweight wool	Cotton or polyester thread
Wool crepe	Cotton or polyester thread
Wool jersey	Cotton or polyester thread
Double knit	Polyester thread
Rayon	Cotton or polyester thread
Lightweight linen	Cotton thread
Linen	Cotton or polyester thread
Fleece	Polyester thread
Velour	Polyester thread
Spandex cotton blend	Polyester thread
Spandex wool blend	Polyester thread

moisture. Collect these as you go. You may be working on a project when one device or the other seems the most appropriate.

Thread

There is one important thing to say about thread: Buy the good stuff. Whether you buy silk thread, cotton thread, polyester thread, or rayon thread, make sure it is of good quality; don't buy junky stuff. It may look like a bargain, but the hassle to use it is not worth the savings. Cheap thread breaks and separates during sewing, so avoid it.

There are many good brands of thread available: Coats & Clark Dual Duty, Swiss Metrosene, Guterman, Molyneke, and Tire.

tip

As a general rule, use polyester thread when you are working on fabric that stretches. Use silk thread whenever possible for basting.

Charts exist that list what thread to use with what fabric, and books on fabric feature this information. For those just starting out, see the chart on the facing page to determine which thread works best for easy fabrics.

Rulers

There are at least three rulers every sewer needs to have. The first is a metal yardstick. The second is a transparent ruler like the C-Thru ruler, and the last is a 6-in.-long seam guide.

Pressing tools

The essential list of pressing tools includes an iron, an ironing board with a good cover, and a press cloth or two.

Let's start with the iron. If you don't have an iron that steams (not drips sort-of-hot water but really steams), you don't have an iron good enough for sewing. Look for a heavy iron with metal parts—you're more likely to get steam than drips.

I have a new cotton duck cover on my ironing board (it has been 10 years since my last new one). I washed the old cover, put it back on the

An iron that steams is essential. You can add other pressing tools as your skills progress. From left to right: pressing boards/tools, sleeve roll, press cloths, and ham and ham holder.

ironing board, then put the new one on top; I like a thick surface that I can stick pins in.

Press cloths can be packaged ones from the sewing notions department or 100% cotton diapers. I use a press cloth to prevent fusible interfacing from sticking to the bottom of my iron as well as to prevent fabric from being marred by steam and heat.

■ BEYOND THE BASIC TOOLS

The more you sew, the more you will become aware of the world of sewing tools that is available. Treat yourself to a new gadget from time to time, and add to your collection as the need arises. The following tools and equipment are things you may want to consider adding to your tool kit.

Rotary cutters

A rotary cutter is a fast, sharp tool for cutting. It is too fast and too sharp if you are just beginning to sew. Once you find yourself sewing a lot or if you are a quilter, you may want to use one. This pizza cutter for fabric has to be used in conjunction with a special mat or it will cut and mar the surface underneath the fabric. I consider a 1-yd.-long mat to be the minimum length you'll need for garment cutting.

Using a rotary cutter is the best way to cut slinky, slippery, and silky fabrics. When you are ready to sew these fabrics, you may be ready to give this tool (and mat) a try.

More pressing tools

Besides irons, there are all sorts of pressing tools available to the home sewer. My list includes a clapper, a sleeve board, a June Tailor board, a ham, and ham holder (see the photo on p. 15).

A clapper is a 3-in. by 8-in. piece of hardboard with curved edges that is used for flattening edges. A sleeve board allows you to press long seams easily, but a rolled-up towel can work just as well.

A June Tailor board is a wooden pressing device used for pressing collars and facings. There are several other wooden pressing tools available that serve this function.

A ham is actually a ham-shaped form that prevents curves in a garment (such as darts) from being pressed flat. The ham holder is the device that keeps the ham from rolling off the ironing board.

Above the basic level are advanced pressing devices: presses, which come in several varieties, and professional gravity-feed irons. Presses feature two heated plates that are lowered to meet each other and press fabric between them. Also available are steam table-type presses, which consist of ironing board tables that create steam in conjunction with a hot iron that flattens fabrics. Some of the best pressing can be done with professional irons, with gravity-fed water providing lots of steam.

You can spend anywhere from $75 to $140 on a good basic iron, but the advanced devices will demand several hundred dollars.

■ CHOOSING A PATTERN

Patterns are the blueprints for the garments we sew. Most of the time, we choose garments from the pictures in pattern books and on pattern envelopes. There is a great deal of information on the pattern envelope that is actually more descriptive than the picture.

But before you buy a pattern, you need to gather some information.

Take your measurements

First, you need to take basic measurements of yourself. These need to be honest measurements, and you don't have to show them to anybody. When you take these measurements,

TAKING YOUR MEASUREMENTS

High bust or chest

Full bust

Waist

High hip (3 in. to 5 in. below waist) and distance from waist

Full hip and distance from waist (usually 7 in. to 9 in. from waist)

hold the tape measure taut but not tight against the body. You don't want to be too loose with the measurements. Regardless of the numbers, clothes that fit look good, so don't cheat.

Take your bust (or for you guys out there, your chest) measurement, measured around the fullest part of your bust or chest. Next, ladies take your high bust measurement around the upper chest and under the arms. Take your waist measurement, then the full hip, which is measured around the widest part of you between your waist and knees. Follow this measurement with the distance between where you take your full hip measurement and your waist. Last, take your high hip measurement. This is typically 3 in. to 5 in. below the waist, where your hips or tummy get round. Take the distance from the high hip to your waist as well.

Examine the pattern envelope

The second step in choosing a pattern is to examine the information on the pattern envelope (see the photo on p. 18).

On the front of the envelope is the fashion picture, the pattern number, and the size or range of sizes in the envelope. It is important to look beyond the fashion drawing to the line drawing of the garment. Each pattern company will place the line drawing in different locations on the envelope, but this will give you a better description of the garment than the fashion drawing.

The line drawing not only outlines the garment but also outlines the shape of the pieces. You will know how many seams there are in

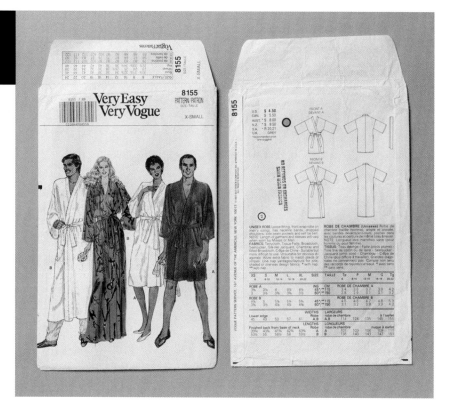

each garment piece, where the seams are, and if there are details such as darts.

Look for the description of the garment. The pattern may simply say, "Very loose fitting," or it may give a full description, "Loose fitting,

> **tip** *Many easy garments are loose fitting, which often means oversized or, to put it bluntly, baggy. It is easy to be disappointed when a T-shirt or pull-on pants turns out to be bigger than you think it will be, when it is actually as described. Be prepared: Loose-fitting garments are baggy.*

lined, below-hip jacket has collar, collar band, forward shoulder seams, shoulder pads, flaps, welt pockets, back vents, long, two-piece sleeves, and concealed button closing."

For additional information about the garment you want to make, look for "finished lengths" or "pattern measurements" or "widths/lengths." This is the information that will tell you how wide the bottom of each pants leg is, how wide a jacket is at the bottom edge, and how full a skirt will be when finished. Pay attention to the finished lengths if you are short or tall. This will give you some idea how much too long or short the garment is going to be and how much you will have to adjust the amount of yardage you need to buy.

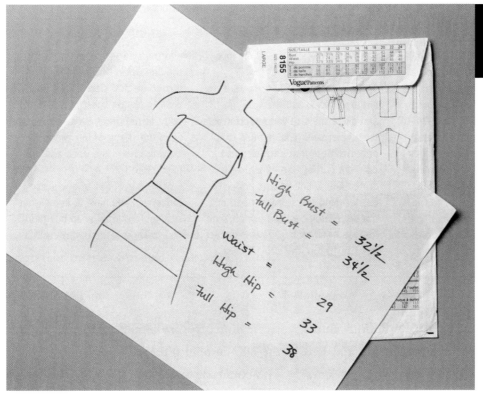

Between the information you get from the line drawing, the written description, and the pattern measurements, you should have a good idea of what kind of project you are choosing. The more seams and details, the more difficult the project will be. The garment widths and lengths will cue you that alterations may be needed, and the description of the garment may steer you to another pattern that is more what you want.

Find the right pattern size

Next, you must determine the pattern size to buy. Forget everything you know about buying ready-to-wear; don't assume that you are a size 10 pattern just because you have never bought anything but a size 10 in ready-to-wear since you were 16 years old. Chances are you won't be a size 10 pattern. You are entering the foreign country of patterns now, and the numbers are different here.

Each of the major pattern companies bases its pattern sizes on a "sloper," which is the standard shape for that company. The back pages of the pattern catalogs tell you the measurements for each pattern size. Be aware that each pattern company's sloper is different and may not have been adjusted for all the years the company has been in business.

Take out your list of measurements and compare it to the measurement chart on the pattern envelope or the size charts in the back pages of the pattern catalog (see the photo above).

read them. The instructions contain lots of information about the garment you are making and even about sewing in general.

Read the instructions

The pattern instructions include line drawings of the garment and the pattern pieces. Typically, there is a short glossary of sewing terms, instructions on how to lay out the pattern pieces, information on which pieces to interface or line if that's appropriate, and the step-by-step sewing process you will follow to construct the garment.

Find and cut the pieces

On the instructions, note the list of pattern pieces; most are numbered as well as labeled. If there is more than one garment in the pattern,

the instructions will indicate which pattern pieces are needed for each garment. Find the pieces you need for the garment you are making and cut them out, following the line for your size. Cut the pieces exactly on the cutting lines—don't leave any tissue. It will be easier to cut the fabric if you do this. After cutting, set the pieces aside.

Identify the pattern symbols

Looking at the pattern pieces, you will see that each piece has a variety of symbols (see the illustration below). First, a straight line with an arrow at each end indicates the grainline. If the piece is to be cut on the fold, the symbol on the pattern will be along the side to be placed on the fold. The symbol for this is a straight line with two arrows bent toward the

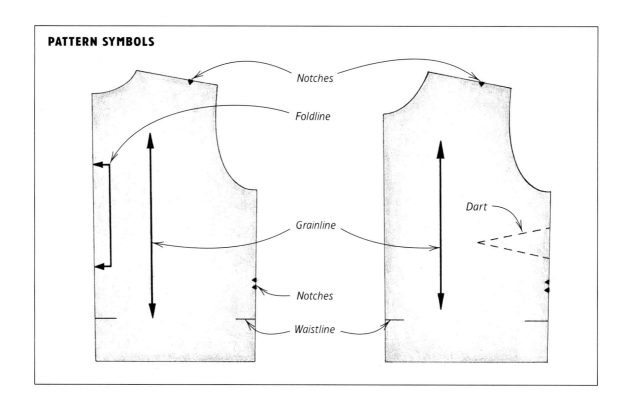

PATTERN SYMBOLS

Notches

Foldline

Grainline

Notches

Waistline

Dart

edge of the pattern piece, pointing to the fold. Some pattern companies provide written instructions rather than symbols. "Place on fold of fabric" will be printed along the edge that is to be placed on the fold.

Other symbols to look for include notches on the edges of the pattern pieces and large or small dots or a combination of both. More complicated patterns have large and small dots, squares, and triangles. Notches indicate match-points along the edges of the seams. Dots and other small shapes can also indicate match-points but these are generally away from the edge. On tops, two small, adjacent dots typically indicate the shoulder. On skirts, the same mark might indicate the side. The glossary section of the pattern instructions will define the basic symbols: notches, foldline, and grainline. The others are referred to in the sewing instruction section of the pattern instructions.

Lay out the pattern pieces

Referring again to the pattern instructions, locate the section for laying out the pattern pieces on the fabric. Find the layout that pertains to the garment style and size you are making, as well as to the width of your fabric. It may take a bit of time to figure out the drawing. Just as the right side of the fabric is often shaded differently from the wrong side, the right side of a pattern piece is also shaded differently from the wrong. The pattern also indicates selvages and fold of fabric, but there is often an abbreviation for these terms (S/L for selvage; F/L for foldline). Note the way the

tip *If the layout section of the pattern instruction sheet becomes confusing, circle the drawing of the layout you need. This will help you stay focused on the correct drawing.*

patterns are laid out: Are the tops all at one end? Where are the grainlines?

For ease in laying out the pattern on the fabric, work on a flat table that is at least 1 yd. long. The fabric is typically folded in half the long way, which means along the lengthwise grain. Line up the selvage edges and make the fabric lie flat. The cut ends are not always even, so sometimes you have to gently tug the fabric on the diagonal to flatten it, especially if the fabric has been washed and dried (see the photo on p. 24). If needed, pin the selvages together to help you keep the fabric even.

Prepare the entire length of fabric even though your work surface may not be very long. Roll up or fold up the pinned fabric that would otherwise drape off your table while your work on the unpinned section. The

tip *Orient the pattern instructions so that they correspond to the way you have your fabric. If the fold of your fabric is on the left, turn the instructions so that they match the way your fabric is placed. Then you are ready to place the pattern pieces on the fabric.*

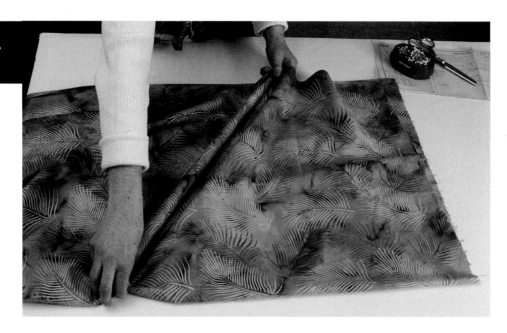

If the fabric doesn't lie flat, tug it a bit to even it out.

weight of fabric hanging off the edge of a table can distort the fabric. I use a stool to catch the excess at one end; the back of a chair would work well, too.

Pin the pieces

When pinning, work with one pattern piece at a time. Place the pattern piece on the fabric, find one end of the grainline, and then pin it through all thicknesses of the fabric. Measure from the pin to the selvages (see the top photo on the facing page). Find the other end of the grainline, then make sure the distance is the same between the grainline and the selvages and pin. Once you have the grain-

> **tip** *When pinning, it is important that the pattern stays flat on the fabric and that you don't pin outside the lines.*

line right, you can pin the rest of the pattern piece—first pinning the corners, then every 5 in. or so. Everybody pins differently—I pin pointing out.

For a pattern piece that is positioned on the fold, pin along the folded edge before smoothing out and pinning the remainder of the piece. You do not have to measure to the selvages to make sure the grain is straight with pieces placed on the fold. Since you were careful folding the fabric exactly in half, the fold is parallel to the selvages.

Work from one end of the fabric to the other, pinning all the pieces and folding up the fabric as you go (see the bottom photo on the facing page).

It is important to note that not all patterns are laid out on fabric that is folded in half lengthwise. In some layouts, the pattern pieces are positioned on a single thickness of fabric and cut twice, while on others pattern pieces are

To line up a pattern piece along the lengthwise grain, measure from each arrow to the selvage (top). A piece that is placed along the foldline is placed exactly on the folded edge (bottom).

Pin the corners and every 5 in. or so in between. Roll up the work as you go, pinning all the pieces before cutting.

placed on partially folded fabric. The layouts provided in the pattern instructions will indicate what to do. If you are confused, call that sewing friend of yours or go back to the fabric store and ask for help.

In any event, whenever possible, lay out and pin all the pattern pieces before you cut any of them.

Cut out the fabric pieces

Cutting the pattern pieces is straightforward. Cut right along the edge of the pattern piece (which is why you should cut excess tissue away). Don't take short, choppy cuts but rather use the length of the scissor blade. I am right-handed, so I use my left hand to keep the fabric flat, and I turn the excess fabric out of the

way as I cut around each pattern piece (see the photo above). I also move around the table, keeping the fabric flat and not pulling it toward me, which might distort the layout.

■ MARKING THE PIECES

After cutting all the pieces, transfer the markings from the pattern piece to the fabric. For the notches, I make a small snip—*not* a V cut, just a ⅛-in.-long snip—on the edge (see the photo at right). I know some very good sewers who never snip the edges but rather use chalk or thread to mark the notches. If you do choose to snip, remember to keep the snips small.

For marks that are inside the edges—the dots, squares, and triangles, as well as darts and pleats—you have the choice of making tailor tacks or using other marking devices. (See "Tailor Tacks" on the facing page.)

Mark notches with small ⅛-in. snips.

■ INTRODUCTION TO THE SEWING MACHINE

Just as you acquainted yourself with the instructions before you laid out the pattern pieces, so too should you acquaint yourself with your sewing machine before you start to use it.

To make tailor tacks, take a 24-in.-long piece of thread that is contrasting in color from the fabric you are using and fold it in half. Thread the two ends through the eye of the sewing needle so that there are four threads on the threaded needle. Do not knot the thread. Take a stitch where you want the mark to be—for example, at the tip of a dart, centered on a dot or triangle, or at the end of a buttonhole—through the pattern piece and both thicknesses of fabric. Cut the thread, leaving a tail that is at least ½ in. long on each side of the stitch (see the top photo). Pull the pattern away, then carefully separate the fabric pieces. Snip the threads, being careful not to cut the fabric (see the bottom photo). You will then have a thread mark on all four sides of the two fabric pieces.

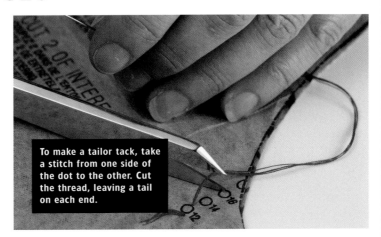

To make a tailor tack, take a stitch from one side of the dot to the other. Cut the thread, leaving a tail on each end.

Carefully separate the fabric pieces and cut the stitch between them.

Finding your way around

The manual that accompanies each machine contains diagrams and instructions for threading the upper part of the machine and the bobbin. A simplistic explanation of a stitch is that a thread from the top of the machine comes together with a thread from the bottom onto the surface of the fabric. Therefore, you need thread in the bobbin casing and thread in the top of the machine in order for your machine to work.

Familiarize yourself with the parts of the machine: Find the presser foot lifting/lowering lever. Find the fly wheel. Find the buttons and knobs for lengthening and shortening the stitches, for backing up, for making a zigzag stitch and adjusting the width of the zigzag, and for moving the needle to the left and right of center. Most modern machines include these features, which will be described in the manual. If you are unsure about your machine or if you have an old machine without a manual,

PINNING FOR MACHINE SEWING

If you will be sewing by machine, pin your fabric pieces so that you can take the pins out as you sew. You must never sew over pins regardless of what anyone says. It's not good for the pins, the needle, or the machine. I pin parallel to the edge, with pins pointing toward the direction in which I'm sewing.

When you are sewing pieces together on the sewing machine, there are a few basics to remember:

• Pin the ends, notches, and at 4-in. to 5-in. intervals.

• Pin so that you can take the pins out as you sew.

• Pin so that the ⅝-in. seam allowance you are sewing is on the right and will pass through the small opening in the sewing machine.

• Pin so that the biggest part of the pieces you are sewing will be on the left of the machine and can lie on the table as the seam is being sewn.

---

visit the dealer where you bought the machine for instructions or find a good repairperson who can acquaint you with your machine.

Practicing sewing

Practice sewing straight lines on scraps of fabric. Although some machines have line markings that indicate the standard ⅝-in. seam allowance and other common distances from the needle, it helps to have an more obvious visual aid for a seam guide. My favorite visual aid is a Post-It note, which can be placed along the ⅝-in. line. A rubber band slipped over the free-arm of the sewing machine and placed along the ⅝-in. line is another alternative. There are also devices that attach to the machine that work well.

To practice, take two pieces of fabric that are the same length. Pin them right sides together along the ⅝-in. seamline, matching the edges you are pinning. You will almost always sew right sides together and will almost always sew a ⅝-in. seam, so it's best to practice this way, too. I recommend pinning each end and every

4 in. to 5 in. in between (although your scrap may not be this long). (See "Pinning for Machine Sewing" above.)

Check the stitch length on the machine, and adjust it to be in the range of 10 to 12 stitches per inch, or 2.5 on metric machines. Most sewing will be done in this range.

Place the fabric pieces under the presser foot with both edges along the seam guide. With your hand, turn the fly wheel and lower the needle into the fabric, then lower the presser foot. Make sure both the bobbin thread and the needle thread are placed to the back of the machine (see the top left photo on the facing page). It is a good idea to keep your fingers on the thread tails until you have sewn a couple of stitches. With my older machine especially, I find that this prevents getting wads of thread under the fabric at the beginning of the seam.

Starting at the edge of the fabric, sew a few stitches, then lock the stitches by taking a couple of stitches backward before continuing forward (see the bottom left photo on the facing page). A stitch or two is all you need to lock

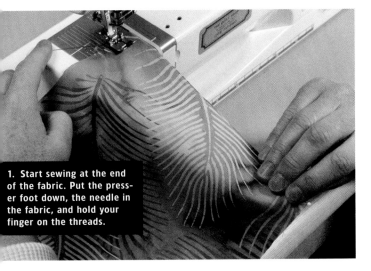

1. Start sewing at the end of the fabric. Put the presser foot down, the needle in the fabric, and hold your finger on the threads.

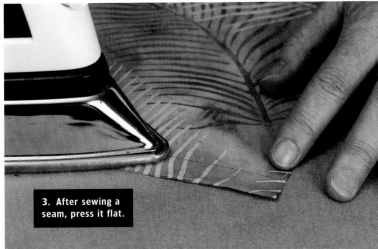

3. After sewing a seam, press it flat.

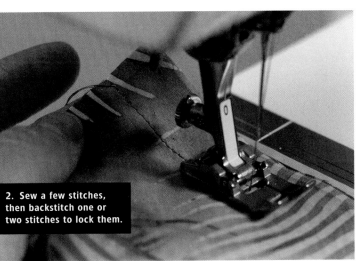

2. Sew a few stitches, then backstitch one or two stitches to lock them.

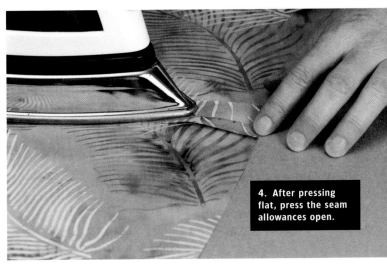

4. After pressing flat, press the seam allowances open.

the stitching. More than that adds thickness to the seamline, and if you had to redo the seam, you would have a lot of stitches to take out.

Sew to the end of the fabric, and again lock the stitches with a backstitch or two. Lift the needle out of the work by turning the fly wheel with your hand, lift the presser foot, and pull the work away from the machine leaving a thread tail. Cut the tail in half so that the machine has a tail and the fabric piece does, too.

Pressing

After you have sewn a seam, it is a requirement that you press it. Press the seam flat, then press the seam open from the wrong side, and finally press the seam flat from the right side (see the top and bottom photos at right above).

You are now ready to work on a garment! The information contained in this chapter is the foundation for the sewing that is ahead.

skirts and pants

■ ■ 2 ■

Skirts and pants can be paired with T-shirts or turtlenecks, under jackets or sweaters. One simple skirt or a good pair of pants can look different every day of the week when worn with a different top. There are about a dozen differ-ent techniques you need to know to construct these essential wardrobe pieces. I'll examine all of them.

Pattern: Burda 2849
Fabric: Cotton/linen
Needle: 80/12 H
Thread: Mettler
silk-finish cotton
Straight stitch, 2.5
Modification:
Drawstring with
elastic added

■ THE EASIEST: PULL-ONS

Some of the easiest garments to make are pull-on skirts, pants, and shorts. Rather than using zippers or button openings, pull-ons, as you can guess, have elastic waistbands that expand. The pattern envelope indicates that the garment has a casing with elastic, and the line drawings usually show a cinched-in waist. Pull-ons can be baggy or relatively close to the body. Check the garment description and the pattern measurements on the pattern envelope.

Marking the fabric

After you have cut out the fabric, look for the markings on the pattern pieces that you need to transfer to the fabric (see p. 26). Specifically, look for the notches, which are the small triangles on the edges of the pattern pieces, and any dots. Although there are no special markings for the casing, mark the casing by making small snips or marks at the waistline in the seam-allowance area.

Take the pattern pieces off the fabric. If it's hard to tell the right side of the fabric from the wrong side, mark the wrong side with peel-and-stick labels or make an X in chalk. Repin each pattern piece to the fabric until you are ready to use it.

Constructing side-seam pockets

If your pull-on skirt or pants has side-seam pockets, then they should be constructed first. Side-seam pockets are made by attaching the pocket pieces to the front and back garment pieces, sewing the side seams above and below the pocket, then sewing around the pocket bag. Most pull-on garments have pocket pieces that are shaped so that the top of the pocket is closed when the waistband is added. Construct side-seam pockets as follows.

1. After cutting the pocket pieces and garment pieces, transfer all markings to the fabric, especially the markings that indicate where the pocket opening will be.

2. With right sides together and using the notches as your guide, position and pin one of the pocket pieces right sides together on the garment front piece, and one pocket piece

---

CONSTRUCTING
A PULL-ON SKIRT

- Cut out the fabric pieces.
- Transfer the markings from the pattern to the fabric.
- Construct side-seam pockets (optional).
- Sew the seams.
- Construct the casing.
- Hem the skirt.

CONSTRUCTING
PULL-ON PANTS

- Cut out the fabric pieces.
- Transfer the markings from the pattern to the fabric.
- Construct side-seam pockets (optional).
- Sew the side seams and inseams.
- Sew the curved crotch seam.
- Construct the casing.
- Hem the pants.

SIDE-SEAM POCKETS—ATTACHING POCKET PIECES TO GARMENT PIECES

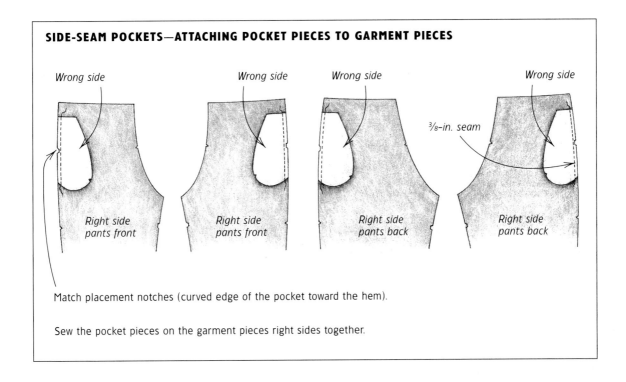

Match placement notches (curved edge of the pocket toward the hem).

Sew the pocket pieces on the garment pieces right sides together.

right sides together on the garment back piece (see the illustration above).

3. Sew the pocket pieces to the garment pieces using a ⅜-in. seam allowance, rather than a ⅝-in. one. A ⅝-in. seam allowance would be right along the garment side seam, creating bulk. Using a narrower seam allowance to attach the pockets eliminates this bulk.

4. Press each pocket piece out, toward the side of the garment, then press the seam allowances in the same direction.

5. With right sides together, place the garment front on the garment back, matching the top and bottom edges of the garment and the notches along the seam. The pocket pieces should line up as well. Sew from the top of the garment to the dot or mark indicating the top of the pocket opening. Next, using a ⅝-in. seam allowance, sew from the dot or mark indicating

SIDE-SEAM POCKETS— SEWING THE SIDE SEAM

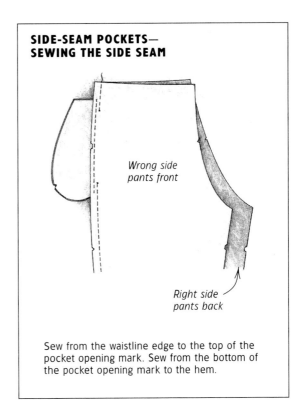

Sew from the waistline edge to the top of the pocket opening mark. Sew from the bottom of the pocket opening mark to the hem.

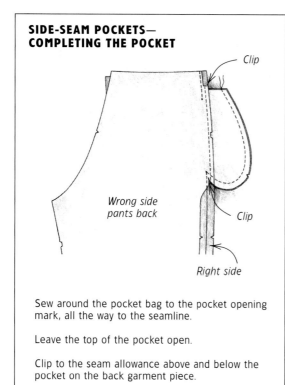

**SIDE-SEAM POCKETS—
COMPLETING THE POCKET**

Clip

*Wrong side
pants back*

Clip

Right side

Sew around the pocket bag to the pocket opening mark, all the way to the seamline.

Leave the top of the pocket open.

Clip to the seam allowance above and below the pocket on the back garment piece.

the bottom of the pocket opening to the hem. Lock the stitches in place when you start and stop stitching by backstitching at the beginning and end of each line of stitching.

6. While the garment pieces are in this position, complete the pocket by sewing around the pocket pieces, starting at the top of the pocket and continuing around the curve of the pocket to the bottom of the opening (see the illustration above). Sew across the seam that attaches the pocket piece all the way to the opening; don't stop at the seam or there will be a little hole for your earrings to fall through.

7. Clip the back seam allowances above and below the pocket pieces. By doing this just on the back piece, the pocket will fall toward the front of the garment where you want it.

Sewing seams

Sewing the seams is most of the work in assembling a pull-on garment. Seams are easy to sew, and you can try on the garment when you're finished.

SKIRT SEAMS When sewing a skirt, you should pin all the seams before you sew. Pin the fabric pieces right sides together, matching the top and bottom edges and any notches along the seam. Pin every 4 in. to 5 in. along the length of the seam.

If there are only two seams in a skirt, I pin both, then sew both. If there are four seams, I pin all four before sewing.

Next, sew the seams, locking the stitches in place at the beginning and end of each seam by backstitching a few stitches. Press the seams after sewing, first flat, then open on the wrong side and finally on the right side of the fabric.

The skirt is ready for the casing. If you try it on now, it will look big and rectangular, maybe even too big, but the elastic in the casing will change that.

PANTS SEAMS Pull-on pants are slightly more complex than pull-on skirts since there are side seams and inseams for each leg. After removing the pattern pieces from the fabric, place the pants back pieces on a flat surface, right sides up. Place each pants front piece right side down on top of each back piece. Each pants leg is constructed separately, and it's important to end up with a leg made with one back and one front piece.

Creating the side seam is straightforward. Pin the top edges together and the bottom edges together, pin at the notches, then pin at

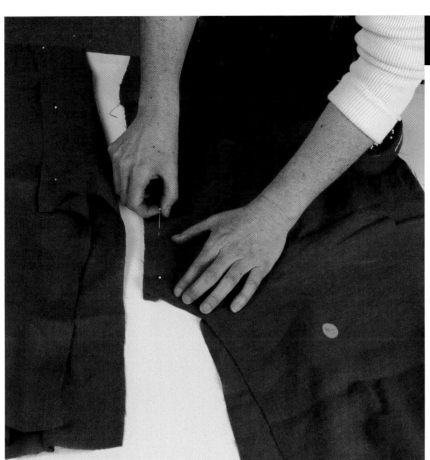

5-in. intervals over the length of the seam (see the photo above).

Next, pin the inseam, which is the shorter leg seam under the crotch curve. You may note that the curved edges of the pant back and the pant front are not shaped the same—the back edge may curve up and the front edge curve out. However, ⅝ in. from the edge—where the seam will be—the edges match (see the illustration at right). This is where you are going to sew. Pin here, pin the bottom edges, then pin at 5-in. intervals over the length of the inseam.

INSEAMS ON PULL-ON PANTS

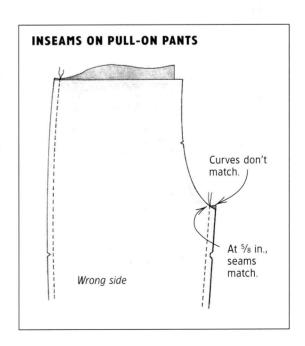

Curves don't match.

At ⅝ in., seams match.

Wrong side

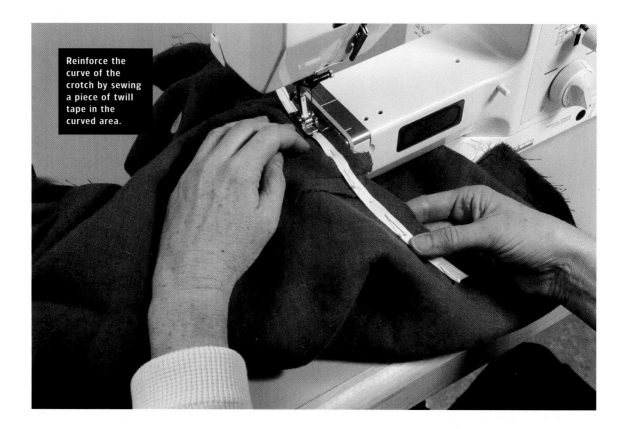

Reinforce the curve of the crotch by sewing a piece of twill tape in the curved area.

Sew the seams, then press. A sleeve board or a rolled towel will help you press the seams open easily.

PANTS CROTCH CURVE To finish a simple pair of pull-on pants or shorts, leave one of the legs inside out and turn the other leg right side out.

Slide the right-side-out leg into the inside-out leg so that the right sides of the fabric pieces face each other. Match and pin the curved crotch seam from waistline edge to waistline edge, then sew a ⅝-in. seam.

It is important to reinforce the bottom of this curved seam, where it is stressed the most by sitting and striding. I recommend reinforcing about 4 in. of the front and 6 in. of the back along this seam. You can simply make a second row of stitches parallel to the first, using a ½-in. seam allowance. Or you can pin a piece of twill tape in the area to be reinforced, then sew the second row of stitches with a ½-in. seam allowance (see the photo above). With either option, trim away the excess ¼ in. of fabric to eliminate bulk.

I typically take an additional step and make a narrow zigzag stitch over the twill tape between the first and second rows of stitches (see the photo on the facing page). Press the seam allowances open above and below the reinforced area.

Finally, pull the garment right side out. The pants are almost finished. They look boxy, but elastic at the waist will fix that.

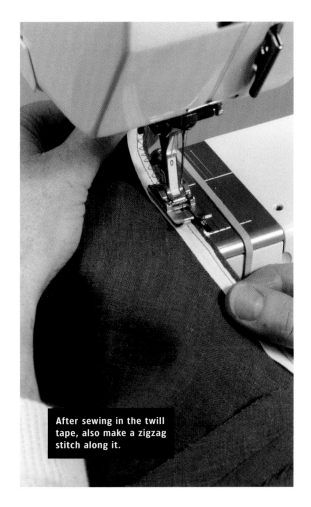

After sewing in the twill tape, also make a zigzag stitch along it.

Making the casing

Elastic is or can be inserted in a casing at the waistline edge of a pull-on garment. There are two basic ways to construct a casing: by folding over fabric at the waistline edge or by adding on a waistband piece.

FOLDOVER CASING The easiest and fastest construction of a waistline casing in a pull-on garment is the foldover casing. You will know that your garment has a foldover casing if there is no band or casing pattern piece or by checking the garment pieces.

To check the pattern pieces, find the waistline. If the pattern extends several inches (not just ⅝ in.) above the waistline, the garment has a foldover casing. If there is only a ⅝-in. seam allowance above the waistline, there is a separate band or casing piece that will be added to the garment.

As outlined in the following steps, the casing is constructed by finishing the raw edge, folding

MARKING THE FOLDOVER CASING

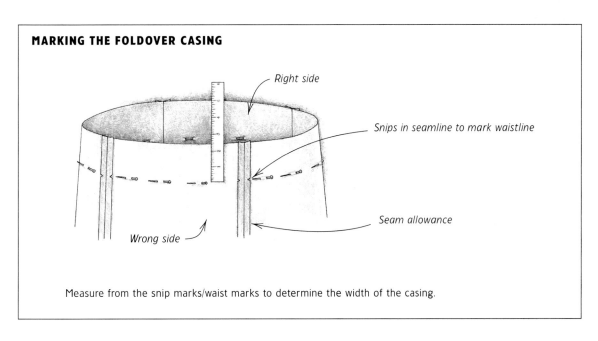

Measure from the snip marks/waist marks to determine the width of the casing.

There are several methods you can use to finish the raw edge of your garment. Here are some suggestions for easy skirts and pants.

Easiest

The easiest edge finish is no finish at all. If you are really in a hurry to finish your project, you can leave the edge unfinished, but don't do this if the fabric ravels.

Easy

Alternatively, you can sew a row of zigzag stitches along this edge, or if you have an overlock machine, serge the unfinished edge (see the illustration below). To finish the edge of a waistline casing or hem—but only if your fabric is light in weight—you can turn ¼ in. of the raw edge of the casing to the wrong side, press, and sew.

Some skill required

You can bind the edge with rayon seam tape. This finish mimics the look of a more couture finish called a Hong Kong finish but is easier to accomplish.

1. Press the seam tape nearly in half so that one side is larger than the other—40/60 rather than 50/50.

2. Slide the tape over the unfinished edge of the casing so that the longer part is on the wrong side of the garment and the shorter side is on the right side. Pin in place.

3. Stitch, using a straight stitch or a zigzag stitch, starting about ½ in. from the unfinished edge (see the illustration on the facing page). After attaching all around the edge, finish by turning under ½ in. of the seam tape and overlapping the unfinished seam tape at the beginning of your work.

Beyond the basics—the Hong Kong finish

Although using rayon seam tape is a fast and easy way to finish a raw edge, if the fabric ravels easily, I will take the extra time to finish the edge with a Hong Kong finish.

A Hong Kong finish is constructed using bias strips, not bias tape that is sold in packages because it is too bulky for this couture finish. I make my own bias strips using lightweight fabric such as lining fabric (see "Make Your Own Bias Strips" on pp. 98-99). For seam finishing, I cut 1¼-in.-wide strips.

1. With right sides together, pin a strip of bias along the edge to be finished. Sew using a ¼-in. seam allowance.

2. Press the bias strip toward the edge, then wrap it over the edge to the wrong side. Pin along the seamline.

3. Stitch in the ditch along the seamline (see "Stitch in the Ditch" on p. 44).

4. On the wrong side, trim away the excess bias. Because it is bias, the edge is not going to ravel, so you can trim close to the stitching line (see the photo on the facing page.)

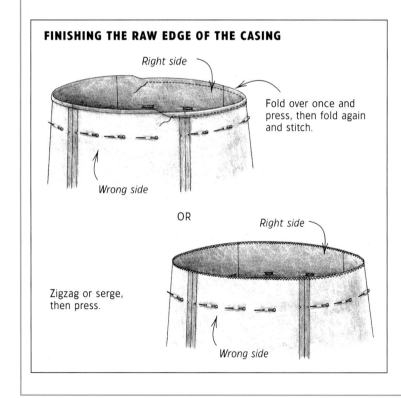

FINISHING THE RAW EDGE OF THE CASING

Right side

Fold over once and press, then fold again and stitch.

Wrong side

OR

Right side

Zigzag or serge, then press.

Wrong side

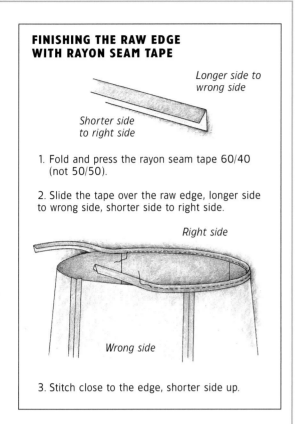

A Hong Kong finish can be used on any raw edge for an elegant couture touch.

the fabric above the waistline in half, sewing the finished edge to the garment leaving an opening for elastic, inserting and adjusting the elastic, then closing up the opening.

1. You may have made little snips or marks at the side seams to mark the casing. If you can't find them, measure the pattern from the waistline to the top of the pattern piece. This is the casing, and you should note the width or mark it on the garment with a pin (see the illustration on p. 37).

2. Before you fold the casing in half, finish the raw edges of the casing. Finishing is more than just aesthetic; it prevents the fabric from raveling, which might cause the casing to come undone. Choose a finishing method from "Finishing Unsewn Edges" at left.

3. Once the edge is finished, use a small ruler and chalk or pins to mark the width of the casing around the waistline edge of the garment. Fold the casing over and pin the top of the finished edge to the chalk/pin line (see the photo on p. 40.)

4. Sew the casing in place along the chalk/pin line, but leave an opening of approximately 3 in. so that you can insert the elastic.

5. Before inserting the elastic, shape it into a circle and overlap the edges the way the elastic will be positioned in the casing. To help keep the elastic in this position and not twisted, mark the two edges that will overlap.

6. Place a large safety pin at one end of the elastic and begin feeding the elastic into the casing. Be careful where there are seam allowances

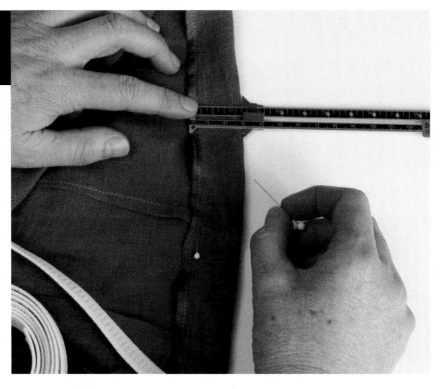

Measure and pin the waist-line casing, making sure that there is enough room for the elastic you are going to use.

tip *You'll need a length of elastic that is about your waist measurement. It's hard to say exactly how long a piece you'll need because different elastics have different amounts of stretch, and some of us like waistbands snug and some like them loose. As a rule of thumb, start with a piece of elastic the same size as your waist. To determine what width elastic you'll need, measure the width of the finished casing. Select elastic that is a bit narrower than the casing is wide to accommodate the thickness of the elastic. You would have to struggle to put 1-in. elastic in a 1-in. casing.*

because you want the elastic to go between them (see the left photo on the facing page).

7. Pull the elastic all the way through the casing, keeping the tail end out. Overlap and pin the ends, matching the marks you made when you started, and then try on the garment. Pull the elastic tighter until the waistline is as snug as you want it, then repin the elastic and take off the garment.

8. Since the edges of the elastic need to overlap each other by only about 1 in., cut off any excess elastic. Pin the overlapping edges together, and pull the casing away from the overlapped edges so that it'll be easy to sew the edges of the elastic together. Sew the elastic using straight stitches, sewing forward and backward for several rows, or zigzag back and forth across the

After marking the ends of the elastic so they don't get twisted, feed the elastic into the casing. The hardest parts are where there are seams, since you don't want the elastic to get stuck under a seam allowance.

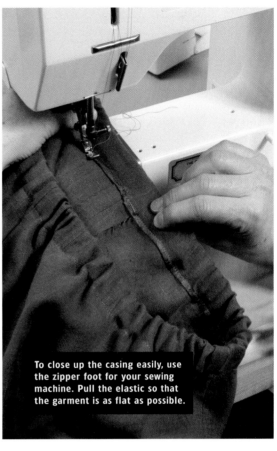

To close up the casing easily, use the zipper foot for your sewing machine. Pull the elastic so that the garment is as flat as possible.

overlap to anchor the two edges together (see the illustration at right).

9. Adjust the gathers on the garment, pin the opening where you inserted the elastic, then sew (see the right photo above).

ADD-ON CASING The add-on casing resembles a sewn-on waistband. A band is seamed to the waistline edge of the garment, the raw edge is finished, then the band is folded over to form a casing, which is attached by stitching in the ditch. Elastic is then inserted in the casing. (See "How Big Is a Casing?" on p. 42.)

STITCHING THE ELASTIC TOGETHER

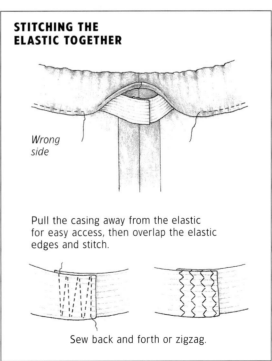

Wrong side

Pull the casing away from the elastic for easy access, then overlap the elastic edges and stitch.

Sew back and forth or zigzag.

HOW BIG IS A CASING?

A pattern will provide you with a piece that forms the add-on casing. If you look at this piece (illustrated below) from one edge to the other, you will see that there is:

• a ⅝-in. seam allowance
• fabric the width of the required elastic plus a bit
• a foldline

• fabric the width of the required elastic plus a bit
• a ⅝-in. seam allowance

The "bits" are the amount of fabric you need to accommodate the thickness of the elastic. If you had a 1-in. casing and you wanted to insert 1-in. elastic, you would have a fight on your hands! There needs to be a bit of room to allow the elastic to move into place.

One of the ⅝-in. seam allowances is attached to the garment; the second is the unsewn edge that will be finished with a zigzag or seam tape. This second edge needs to be at least ¼ in. It doesn't need to be ⅝ in., though, so before you finish the edge, trim away ⅜ in.

SIZE OF THE CASING

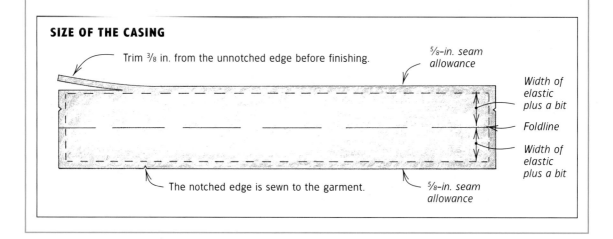

Trim ⅜ in. from the unnotched edge before finishing.

⅝-in. seam allowance

Width of elastic plus a bit

Foldline

Width of elastic plus a bit

The notched edge is sewn to the garment.

⅝-in. seam allowance

---

tip *With elastic casings, it is sometimes difficult to sew the last few inches of stitches since the elastic makes the sewing surface uneven. Sometimes just being aware that it might be difficult is enough to prevent crooked stitches; otherwise use a zipper foot so that you can keep things flat under the presser foot while you are sewing the casing closed.*

1. To construct the add-on casing, begin by sewing the band, right sides together, into a circle. Press the seam open.

2. Place the band around the waistline edge of the garment with right sides together. Pin, then sew the band to the garment using a ⅝-in. seam allowance. Press the band up, above the garment.

3. Next, finish the raw edge of the band. Review "Finishing Unsewn Edges" on p. 38 about finishing the unsewn edge of a foldover casing, and choose one of the methods described.

Pin the casing so that about ¼ in. of it is below the stitching line. (This wool jersey fabric won't ravel, so there is no edge finishing on the casing.)

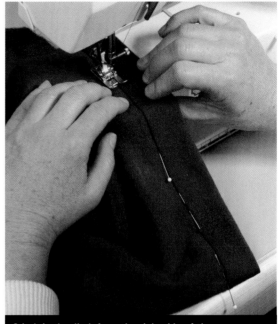

Stitch in the ditch from the right side of the garment. Press the fabric to each side with your fingers so that you can see the ditch.

4. Once the raw edge is finished, press the casing and both seam allowances up toward the top of the garment. Fold the casing over toward the wrong side of the garment so that at least ¼ in. of the finished edge is below the seam that attached the casing. Pin the casing to the garment along the seamline (see the left photo above).

5. Turn the garment over so you are looking at the right side. You are going to sew along the seam attaching the band to the garment, which is called stitching in the ditch. This should be done on the right side of the fabric where you can see the ditch you're stitching in, so transfer the pins to the right side of the garment. As you sew this seam, place your fingers on top of the garment on both sides of the presser foot to keep the seam flat as you sew. I use my

thumb to check that the underside of the area I'm sewing is flat, and I pause to remove pins as I sew (see the right photo above). Sew almost all the way around, leaving a 3-in. to 4-in. opening so that you can insert the elastic.

6. Insert the elastic into the casing, and sew the ends of the elastic together (see the top illustration on p. 44).

7. To finish, pin the unattached area of the casing along the seamline on the right side of the garment. Stitch in the ditch on the right side of the garment. Because there is elastic inside the casing, you have to stretch the area as you sew.

Also because there is elastic inside the casing, the casing is thicker than the rest of the garment, and the presser foot will try to slide toward the flatter side. If you find you are

STITCH IN THE DITCH

Stitch in the ditch is a technique used often in garment construction. In this chapter, the technique is used in constructing a Hong Kong finish and also when attaching a casing or fitted waistband.

Here is how this technique is used in the waistband process. After attaching a skirt to a waistband, sew the short ends of the waistband, turn the band right side out, and fold the band along the foldline. On the wrong side of the garment, a small amount of waistband extends below the seamline. Working from the right side of the garment, pin 1/4 in. of this fabric through all thicknesses along the attachment seam, making sure to catch the little bit on the wrong side of the garment that extends under this seam. Also working from the right side, sew along the seam, keeping it visible by lightly pressing your fingers on both sides.

Some people have a hard time stitching *in* the ditch. The alternative is to sew *next to* the ditch, or seamline, rather than in the ditch.

USING MULTIPLE PIECES OF ELASTIC

Whether your garment has a foldover casing or an add-on casing, the pattern may suggest making two rows of topstitching on the casing and inserting three narrow strips of elastic instead of one, one into each section of the casing. It's a fabulous-looking finish for an elastic-waistband garment. It is, however, one of the greater challenges in life to actually accomplish.

After you insert one piece of elastic, the other two casings collapse. Each additional piece of elastic is harder to insert. There are three remedies: The first is to forget the idea entirely, and make a single casing with a piece of elastic that will fit the width of the casing. Second, if you really want this look, feed all three pieces of elastic into the parallel casings at the same time, working each piece of elastic several inches at a time (see the top illustration at right). It is time-consuming, but it will work.

The third choice is the one that most resembles ready-to-wear elastic-waistband garments: Use the type of elastic that can be stitched through. Stitching horizontally through most elastics cuts the elastic threads, but there is a type you can sew through that has poly-filament threads. To use this elastic, insert it into the casing and finish the casing completely. Then topstitch even rows of stitching through all layers of the casing, stretching the casing as you sew (see the bottom illustration below).

CASINGS WITH MULTIPLE ELASTICS

Wrong side

Feed three narrow elastics at once.

USING SEW-THROUGH ELASTIC

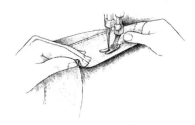

Use a specific type of elastic meant to be sewn through.

Pull tightly from both sides while topstitching.

having problems sewing the casing closed, use a zipper foot to stitch the casing closed in the ditch. (See "Using Multiple Pieces of Elastic" on the facing page.)

Hemming pull-ons

If you have constructed an easy garment on the sewing machine, there is no reason to hem the garment by hand unless you have a real aversion to the look of stitching that shows on the right side of the garment (called topstitching). Hemming by machine appears on all sorts of garments made of all sorts of fabrics, from cotton and linen to silk and wool.

1. To hem a garment, try it on to determine the finished length that you like, then mark it with a pin.

2. Take the garment off, lay it on a flat surface, and line up the garment front and back along the waistline seam. Make an even line of pins around the bottom of the garment to mark the length. The folded-up hem should be even all around the bottom of the garment and can, for a machine-stitched finish, vary from ⅝ in. to 2 in.

3. Consider if and how you want or need to finish the raw edge of the hem, and add the amount needed to do so. You may want to add rayon seam tape on the top of the hem to hide the raw edge, or you may want to fold under ¼ in. to ½ in. For the most part, I fold ½ in. of the raw edge of the hem to the wrong side before stitching in place. This finish looks nice (a typical criteria of mine), and I don't have to worry about raveling.

4. Using a small seam guide, measure the hem depth plus the amount you will turn under or finish (typically ¼ in. to ½ in.), and pin or mark with chalk all the way around the bottom edge of the garment. Cut off any excess fabric.

5. Working on the wrong side of the fabric, fold up the ¼ in. to ½ in. you have allowed to finish the edge, then fold and pin the hem to the depth you measured.

6. Try the garment on again to check the length and to adjust or personalize the hem. (Sometimes it is the shape of our bodies, one hip higher than the other, for instance, that affects the straightness of the hem.)

7. Transfer your pins to the right side of the fabric so that you can remove them easily as you topstitch. Press, but avoid pressing the pins since they leave indents in the fabric.

If you are hemming an A-line skirt or boot-top pants that have some flare, read the "Curved hems" section on p. 76 for some tips on getting your hem to look good without having to overlap little bits of fabric.

8. When topstitching, it is important to sew from the right side of the garment so that you

> **tip** *If folding under ¼ in. to ½ in. makes the hem edge bulky because of the type of fabric you are using, finish the edge by serging, binding with rayon seam tape, or constructing a Hong Kong finish (see "Finishing Unsewn Edges" on p. 38). Knit fabrics don't ravel, so they won't need an edge finish.*

Most sewing teachers will encourage you to finish the seams of your garment. Seam finishes serve two purposes: They look nice and they control raveling. For simple skirts and pants, there are easy options: leaving the seams unfinished, overlocking or zigzagging the seams, and sewing a seam finish.

Leaving seams unfinished

Leaving the seams unfinished is the fastest way to get your garment done. Unless the fabric ravels easily, you can leave the seams unfinished. Also, if you are lining the garment, you don't have to finish the seams because they will be hidden by the lining.

Stitching and pinking

If your fabric ravels easily, you are probably going to want to finish the garment seams to contain the raveling. The easiest seam finish is the one I first learned: stitch and pink.

After completing the seam and pressing it open, sew a line of stitches along each side of the seam allowance. It is important to sew through one layer of fabric only. Line up the sewing machine presser foot with the seamline to help keep your stitches straight. After sewing, cut the edge of the seam allowance with pinking shears (see the photo at right).

Overlocking

Overlocking the seam edges is fast, too. This is accomplished with a serger or with an overlock stitch on your sewing machine. If you don't have a serger or a sewing machine with an overlock stitch, you can use a zigzag stitch along the edge of the seam allowance, which can look really nice and will keep raveling in check. Overlocking results in multiple threads on the seam edges. If the fabric is lightweight, this may leave an impression on the right side of the fabric when pressed, in which case choose a different seam finish.

Using rayon seam tape

Another option is to bind the edge with rayon seam tape. This finish mimics the look of a more couture finish called a Hong Kong finish (see p. 38) but is easier to accomplish.

Press the seam tape nearly in half so that one side is larger than the other—40/60 rather than 50/50. Next, slide the tape over the unfinished edge of the casing so that the longer half is on the wrong side of the seam allowance and the shorter side is on the right side. Pin in place, then stitch. Start sewing about 1/2 in. from the edge of the rayon seam tape. When you have attached the seam tape almost all the way around the unfinished edge, allow enough seam tape to overlap your starting place and cut off any excess. Tuck under the end of the seam tape and overlap the starting place. This allows you to have a nice end without having to seam the tape in a circle.

This seam finish will not work with the polyester seam tape that comes in a package because that tape is permanent press and refuses to stay pressed in half. Polyester tape has a crisper edge, too. Make sure you have rayon seam tape for this finishing technique.

I look at ready-to-wear garments in my favorite stores to see how manufacturers finish seams and take my cues from there. It's nice to know that even expensive skirts and pants have relatively simple seam finishes.

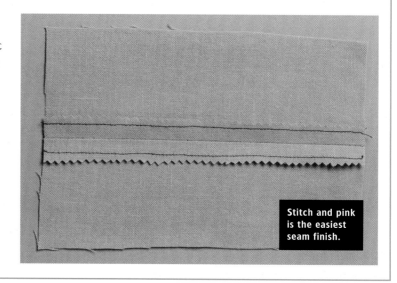

Stitch and pink is the easiest seam finish.

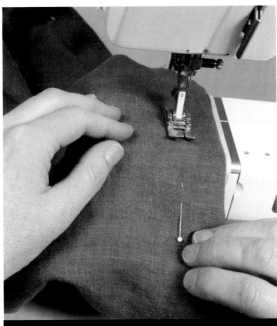

Hemming by machine is quick and easy. A rubber band can be used as a guide to help you keep the hem straight.

know the stitching is straight and looks good. To make sure you are catching the hem, sew a little closer to the edge than the hem is deep. For instance, if you have a 1-in. hem, sew ¾ in. from the edge. There will be a little bit of hem above the stitching line on the wrong side of the fabric (see the photo above).

Inserting drawstrings

Adjustable and comfortable, a fabric drawstring in a casing is an alternative to using elastic. However, drawstrings are most comfortable and don't need to be adjusted quite so frequently when constructed by combining fabric and elastic.

1. Begin by constructing pull-on pants or a skirt to the point of finishing the casing. Before folding over the casing, take out some of the stitching from the center front seam, removing the stitches from the waistline to the foldline. Reinforce the stitching above and below the removed stitches.

2. Fold the casing over and stitch it to the garment all the way around. The split seam is the opening for the elastic, so there is no need to leave any other opening.

3. Next, construct the drawstrings. The finished drawstrings will be as wide as the elastic, which is a bit narrower than the finished width of the casing. You'll need two drawstrings, one for each end of the elastic.

Let's assume we're inserting a ¾-in.-wide drawstring-plus-elastic into a 1-in. casing. In order to make the drawstrings, you need to cut two rectangles of fashion fabric, each 2¾ in. wide by 18 in. to 20 in. long.

4. Fold each rectangle in half, right sides together, and stitch across one short end and down the long end. Trim all seam allowances, then turn drawstring right side out.

5. Take a piece of elastic that is about three-fourths of your waist measurement. Slip the open end of the drawstrings over each end of the elastic. Secure one with multiple rows of straight stitches or zigzag stitches (see the photo on p. 48). Pin the second one in place with a safety pin.

6. Insert the drawstring and elastic into the casing, pulling the drawstring almost all the way out of the split seam. Try on the garment to see how much elastic is needed for the garment to be comfortable and for you to be able to tie the strings nicely.

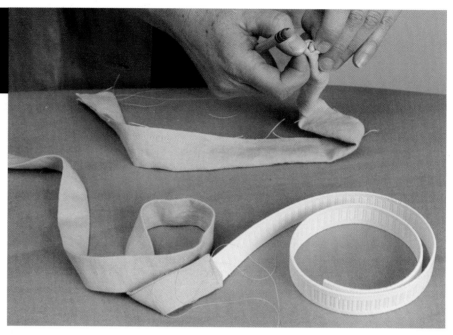

tip *Turning a drawstring right side out can be challenging if your fabric ravels easily. Here are two hints. Hint No. 1: Make the finished drawstring at least 1 in. wide with a ½-in. seam allowance. After sewing, trim across the short end and the corner only, then turn right side out. Hint No. 2: Don't construct a drawstring that is sewn then turned right side out. Instead, start with a rectangle of fabric. Press it in half lengthwise and press each half in half. Unfold and press one end in, refold, then repress along the lengthwise press lines. Topstitch the double-folded edges together.*

7. Pull the pinned end of the drawstring out of the garment, then take off the drawstring and trim any excess elastic. You might have to cut off some elastic and try the garment on one or two more times to get it right. Keep trying, since this is a nice way to finish a pull-on garment. Stitch the second drawstring in place when you like the way the drawstring fits.

An alternative to using a split seam for the drawstring is to construct two buttonholes that are long enough for the drawstring-with-elastic to pass through. The buttonholes should be positioned 3 in. to 4 in. apart in the center front of the garment (see pp. 142-144). This is the better alternative for drawstrings that are bulky and won't pass through a split seam and tie nicely.

■ ADDING ON: SKIRTS AND PANTS WITH ZIPPERS

If you want to make garments that fit closer to the body than pull-on garments, you need to learn a few fitting techniques such as sewing darts and pleats, putting in a zipper, and constructing a waistband. You can also add other touches such as slant-front pockets, hand-finished hems, hooks and eyes, and belt loops.

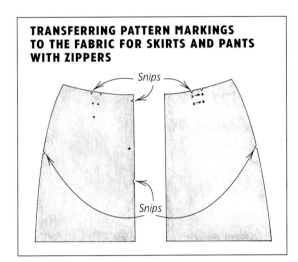

TRANSFERRING PATTERN MARKINGS TO THE FABRIC FOR SKIRTS AND PANTS WITH ZIPPERS

Snips

Snips

Marking the fabric

After you have cut out the fabric, transfer all markings from the pattern piece to the fabric. For garments that fit closer to the body than pull-ons, the markings will include dots that indicate the shape of darts, the length of the zipper, as well as placement of pocket pieces. If the garment has pleats, mark the dots and lines that indicate the location of these details (see the illustration at left).

Transfer the markings from the pattern piece to the fabric using snips for notches, and tailor tacks, chalk, or marking pens for dots and other lines. Mark the waistband by making small snips at the center front and at the overlap/underlap, as well as at the notches that will match it to the waistline edge of the garment.

Take the pattern pieces off the fabric. If you can't tell the right side of the fabric from the wrong side, mark the wrong side with peel-and-stick labels or make a chalk X. Repin the

---

CONSTRUCTING A SKIRT WITH A WAISTBAND

• Cut out the fabric pieces.
• Transfer the markings from the pattern to the fabric.
• Construct darts and pleats.
• Add slant-front pockets (optional).
• Sew the side seams.
• Insert the zipper.
• Add a lining (optional).
• Add the waistband.
• Hem the skirt.

CONSTRUCTING PANTS WITH A WAISTBAND

• Cut out the fabric pieces.
• Transfer the markings from the pattern to the fabric.
• Construct darts and pleats.
• Add slant-front pockets (optional).
• Sew the side seams and inseams.
• Insert the zipper.
• Sew the curved crotch seam.
• Add the waistband.
• Hem the pants.

pattern pieces to the fabric pieces until you are ready to use them.

Sewing darts

Darts are triangles of pinched-out fabric that are stitched down to give a garment shape (see the photo at right). More fabric is pinched out at one end of a dart than another. For instance, more fabric is pinched out at the waist than at the hip. The narrow end of the dart—the dart point—points to the fuller part of the body. In the case of skirts and pants, the darts point to the hips.

MARKING Transfer the shape of the dart from the pattern to the fabric. You can trace the dart onto the wrong side of the fabric using a tracing wheel and paper; you can use tailor tacks or chalk to transfer the markings; or you can use a combination of snips and tailor tacks or chalk marks to transfer the markings.

I use this last method. I make tiny snips at the waistline edge of the garment to indicate the outer edges of the dart. I make tailor tacks at the dart point. If the dart is longer than 4 in., I also make tailor tacks at the midpoint of each side of the dart, marking any small dots that are on the pattern.

SEWING Darts are sewn first in the construction process.

1. To sew a dart in a skirt or pair of pants, fold the fabric right sides together along an imaginary line through the center of the triangular dart.

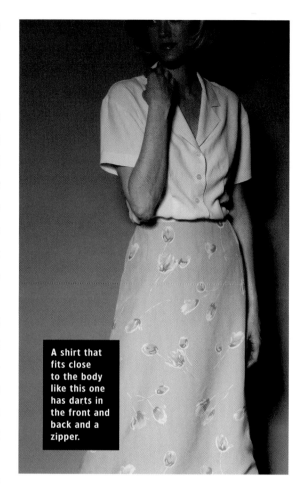

A shirt that fits close to the body like this one has darts in the front and back and a zipper.

2. Match the snips at the waistline edge and pin, then find the dart point, which is where the stitching will end, and pin. Also, find and pin any midpoint marks.

3. Next, imagine a straight line from the snips at the waistline edge to the dart point. Since your body is curved here, a straight line of stitches wouldn't fit smoothly over your hip, so you have to sew a curved line.

To make sewing a curve easier, lightly trace a curved line inside the imaginary straight line with chalk or a pencil (see the top photo on the facing page).

4. Using a regular stitch length, begin sewing at the waistline edge, backstitching one or two stitches to lock the stitches. When you are about ½ in. from the dart point, shorten your stitch length a bit (12 to 14 stitches per inch or 1.75 mm) and continue sewing. Sew off the fabric at the dart point without backstitching. The smaller stitches lock the threads, and there is no extra bulk at the dart point from backstitching (see the photo at right).

PRESSING Press the dart toward the center of the garment. When the darts are on the garment front, press toward the center front; when the darts are on the garment back, press toward the center back. Press, but try not to flatten the curve you have worked hard to sew. If you have a pressing ham, lay the dart over the ham and press (see the photo on p. 52). This helps keep the curve in the dart. If you don't have a ham, press over a towel or hold one side of the garment piece up while you press the other.

> ## tip
> *When you are sewing near a dart point, don't shorten the stitches too much. The rule is never to shorten the stitches so much that you couldn't take them out if you wanted to.*

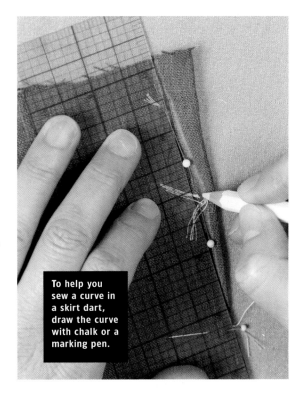

To help you sew a curve in a skirt dart, draw the curve with chalk or a marking pen.

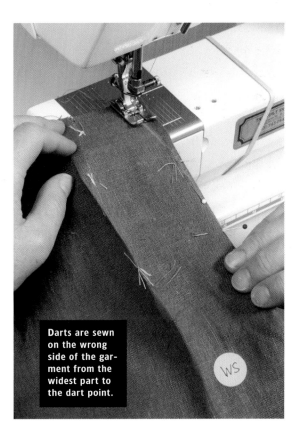

Darts are sewn on the wrong side of the garment from the widest part to the dart point.

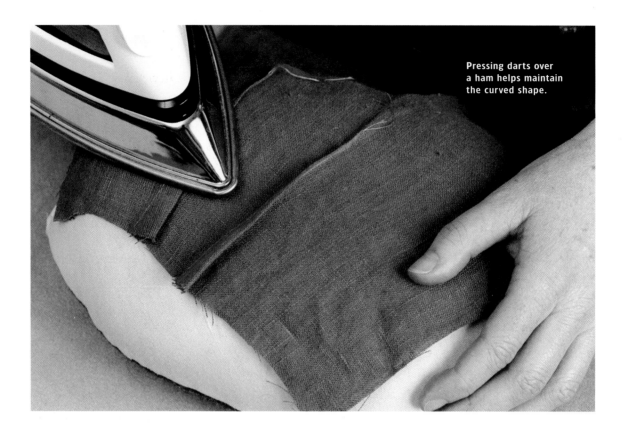

Pressing darts over a ham helps maintain the curved shape.

Sewing pleats

Basic skirts and pants patterns often include pleats as well as darts. Simple, short pleats are easy to construct. Hold off on constructing a fully pleated garment for a future project.

Much like darts, pleats are folded or pinched-out sections of fabric that are used to add fit and shape to a garment. A skirt with front pleats rather than darts has fabric pinched out at the waistline edge, leaving fullness several inches below the waist—at the tummy—where more fullness is needed. Sometimes pleats are stitched down and sometimes they are not.

MARKING THE PLEAT A pattern that features pleats will have distinctive markings. There will be a series of lines, usually with dots of different sizes and arrows or Xs. These are the foldlines and placement lines that constitute the pleat.

Mark the lines, dots, and Xs—whichever combination your pattern has. You can make little snips at the waistline edge to mark the lines and tailor tacks for the dots and Xs. If you wish, you can use different colored thread for the dots and Xs (see the illustration on the facing page).

> **tip** *Practice makes perfect with darts. It's not easy to sew that curved line, so remember it's okay to draw the shape you want to sew.*

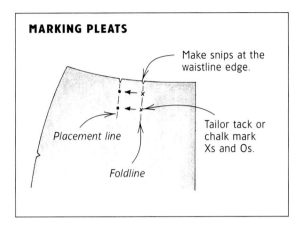

MARKING PLEATS

Make snips at the waistline edge.

Placement line

Foldline

Tailor tack or chalk mark Xs and Os.

CONSTRUCTING THE PLEAT Pleats fold toward the center front of a garment or toward the side seams. To make the pleat, pinch the fabric along one foldline, then bring that foldline to the second, or placement, line, following the direction of the arrows or the pattern instruc-tions. Pin the folded fabric through all thicknesses (see the photo below).

The pattern will instruct you to baste the pleat in place along the waistline edge, which means to machine-stitch with a long stitch (4 to 6 stitches per inch) or a hand stitch. Basted pleats will be permanently anchored when you add the waistband. The pattern then may tell you to stitch the pleat. To do this, sew a line of stitches through all layers of fabric 1 in. to 2 in. down from the waistline edge, making sure you lock the beginning and end of the stitching line with a backstitch or two.

A box pleat is flat across the top, and each side folds under toward the center. This type of pleat is constructed by folding the fabric right sides together, matching the two pleat lines, and stitching along this line for 2 in. to 3 in.

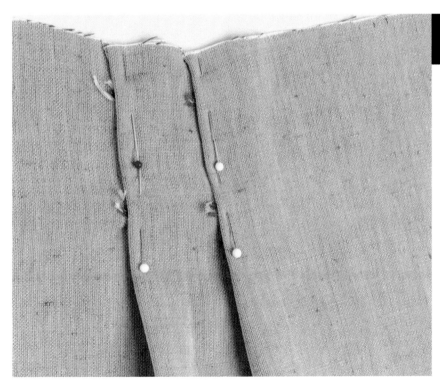

Pin pleats down for an inch or two so that they stay nicely folded.

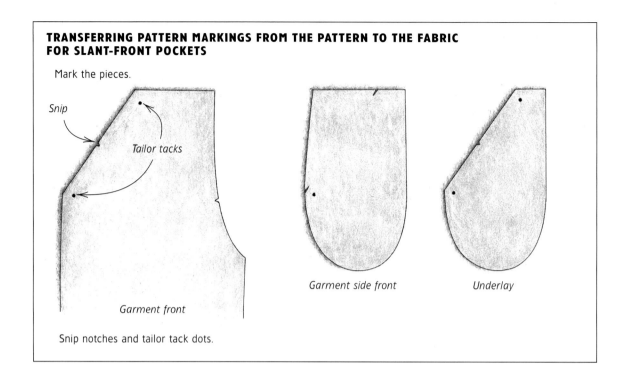

TRANSFERRING PATTERN MARKINGS FROM THE PATTERN TO THE FABRIC FOR SLANT-FRONT POCKETS

Mark the pieces.

Snip

Tailor tacks

Garment front

Garment side front

Underlay

Snip notches and tailor tack dots.

Finish by flattening the pleat, matching the center of the pleat fold to the stitching line.

Pleats in skirts and pants are flattering. They are not any more time-consuming than darts and are not difficult to make once you know what to look for.

Making slant-front pockets

Slant-front pockets are attractive additions to skirts and pants. To make them, you need to familiarize yourself with the pattern pieces and use stay tape. The pattern pieces for a slant-front pocket consist of the garment front and the garment side front, which is also the pocket back. The third piece is the underlay.

1. Begin by making sure you have transferred all the notches and dots from the pattern to the fabric (see the illustration above).

2. Cut a length of stay tape the length of the pocket opening, using the garment front pattern piece to determine how much tape you will need. The word "slant" in slant-front pocket is a clue that these pockets are often on the diagonal, which is off-grain and will stretch out of shape if not stabilized.

3. Position the pocket underlay right sides together on the garment front, matching notches. Pin along the seamline, then pin the stay tape along the seamline. You have the option of basting the tape in place. Next, sew through all layers using a ⅝-in. seam allowance (see the left illustration on the facing page).

4. Press the pocket underlay out, away from the garment front, then press both seam allowances toward the pocket underlay. Next, understitch the seam allowances by sewing both seam allowances onto the pocket under-

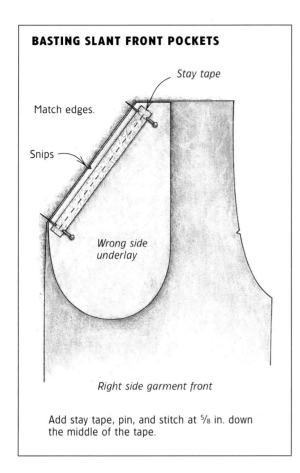

BASTING SLANT FRONT POCKETS

Stay tape

Match edges.

Snips

Wrong side underlay

Right side garment front

Add stay tape, pin, and stitch at ⅝ in. down the middle of the tape.

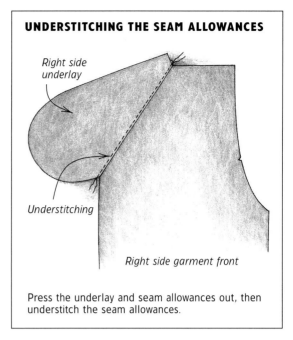

UNDERSTITCHING THE SEAM ALLOWANCES

Right side underlay

Understitching

Right side garment front

Press the underlay and seam allowances out, then understitch the seam allowances.

lay approximately ⅛ in. from the attachment seam (see the right illustration above).

5. Trim, grading the seam allowances so that the seam allowance closest to the top of the garment is the longest.

6. Next, press the underlay in place on the wrong side of the garment. The edge of this diagonal pocket opening is often topstitched. If you choose this detail, topstitch the edge of the pocket opening now.

7. Working from the right side of the garment, position the garment side front piece partly under the pocket/garment front, matching notches along the waistline edge and the side seam. Note that the pocket is not flat but

tip *Grading the seam allowances is a technique to eliminate bulk. To do this, flip the garment into its finished position. You will notice that both seam allowances are right next to each other. Check which of these seam allowances is next to the top side of the garment. This seam allowance should be trimmed a bit (about ¼ in.), but the second seam allowance should be trimmed a lot (about ⅜ in.).*

has some curve to it. Pin or pin and baste the garment side front to the pocket/garment front (see the illustration on p. 56).

8. To complete the pocket bag, fold back the pocket/garment front and match the unsewn, curved edge of the underlay to the unattached

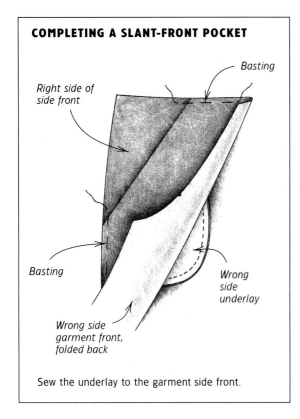

COMPLETING A SLANT-FRONT POCKET

Basting

Right side of side front

Basting

Wrong side underlay

Wrong side garment front, folded back

Sew the underlay to the garment side front.

edges of the garment side front. Sew together using a ⅝-in. seam allowance.

9. Pin and baste the pocket back in position along the waistline edge, then pin or pin and baste the pocket back along the side seam. The side of the pocket will be anchored in the gar-ment side seam, and the top of the pocket will be anchored in the garment waistband.

Inserting zippers

Zipper styles change as garment styles change. When I was learning to sew, centered and lapped zippers were found in ready-to-wear and an invisible zipper was the mark of a homemade look. Now, the reverse is true: Invisible zippers are found in most ready-to-wear garments, while lapped and particularly centered zippers are much less popular.

Sewing all zippers requires the use of the zipper foot that comes with your sewing machine. A special foot is available for inserting invisible zippers, but since it doesn't fit all machines, these instructions are for using a standard zipper foot.

Zippers have various parts, which include the zipper pull, the teeth, and the stop (see the illustration on the facing page). The zipper tape is the woven fabric along each side of the teeth. On many zippers, the weave changes in the middle of the tape or there is a long, visible thread, both of which you can use as sewing guidelines. If the zipper has been fold-

STAY TAPE

Stay tape is a linen or cotton tape, sometimes called twill tape, that is used as a stabilizer, partic-ularly where the fabric is cut off-grain and might stretch. You will find stay tape used along the curve of a crotch seam, along a diagonal pocket opening, along a V-neck, along shoulder seams, and around a waist edge. The tape is narrow—¼ in. or ⅜ in. wide. If you don't have any linen or cotton tape on hand, you can use the selvage edge of a piece of lining. One advantage of using lining fabric is that you are not limited to the few colors in which stay tape is available (white, green, and black).

PARTS OF A ZIPPER

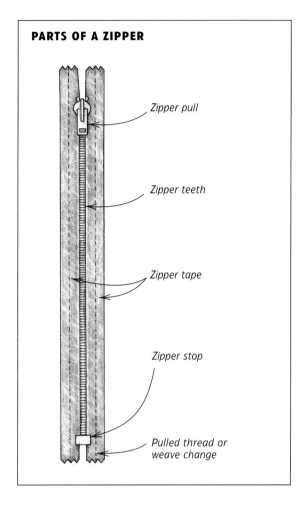

Zipper pull

Zipper teeth

Zipper tape

Zipper stop

Pulled thread or weave change

ed in a package, press it flat before using. You can press right on the teeth—the plastic that is used to manufacture zippers is not the kind that will melt when you press it.

CENTERED ZIPPERS The most basic zipper insertion is the centered application. This type of zipper is characterized by two visible stitching lines on the right side of the garment, which are parallel to each side of the zipper teeth.

1. To begin this zipper application, sew the ⅝-in. seam allowance closed from the waistline edge to the end mark using a long basting stitch (see the photo below). Pull the work out of the machine, leaving a thread tail, then finish sewing the seam using a regular stitch length, backstitching at the beginning and end of the line of stitching.

2. Press the seam allowances open, and lay the work on a flat surface wrong side up. Next, position the zipper right side down, centered on the seam allowance with the teeth along the

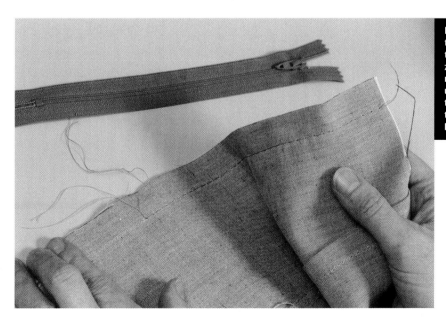

Prepare a seam for a centered zipper by basting to the dot or mark where the zipper ends and sewing the rest of the seam with a regular stitch length. Be sure to stop and leave a tail of thread at the end of the basted seam.

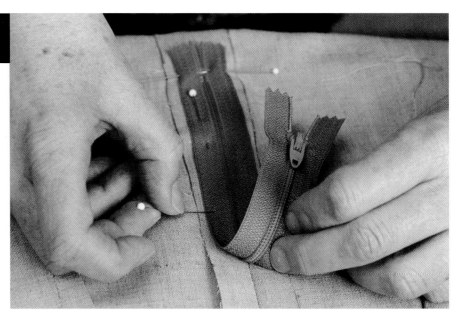

Center the zipper teeth on the seamline and pin the zipper in place.

Since you are going to sew on the right side of the garment, switch the pins to the right side. Pin close together so the zipper doesn't move around.

seam, and turn the zipper pull up. Pin the zipper in place through all thicknesses on each side of the zipper teeth, using the pulled thread or the change in weave in the center of the zipper tape as a guide (see the top photo above).

3. Turn the work over, and repin on the right side of the garment while removing the pins on the wrong side (see the bottom photo above). Be careful to keep the zipper in position when you flip the pins.

4. Position the garment in the sewing machine at the bottom of the zipper at the seam. Before you sew, make sure you have changed from the all-purpose presser foot to the zipper

foot and that the needle is between the zipper teeth and the zipper foot.

5. Sew across the bottom of the zipper on one side of the seam, backstitching to lock the threads in place. Sew several stitches until you are in line with the pins, then stop with the needle down in the work or turn the fly wheel by hand to move the needle down. Lift the zipper foot and turn the work, lower the foot, and resume sewing along the side of the zipper. Follow the line of pins to the waistline edge of the zipper, and backstitch at the end of the line of stitching (see the illustration below). Try to keep the stitches as straight as possible when you are sewing past the zipper pull.

6. Put the garment back into the machine, again at the bottom of the zipper. You are going to sew along the second side of the zipper, so switch the needle position or the foot position so that once again the needle is closer to the zipper teeth than the zipper foot is.

7. Sew as you did the first side: start at the seam and sew across the bottom of the zipper, stopping with the needle down, lifting the zip-

TOPSTITCHING A CENTERED ZIPPER

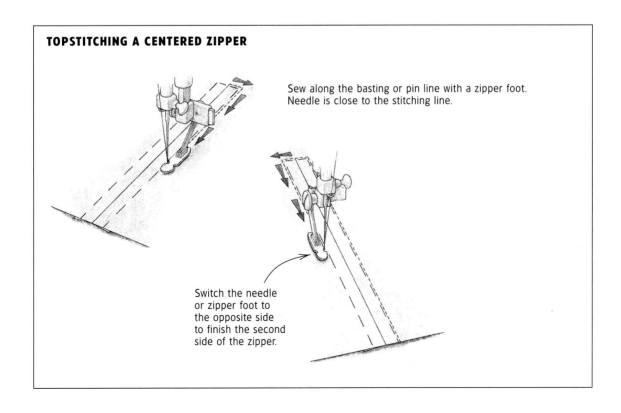

Sew along the basting or pin line with a zipper foot. Needle is close to the stitching line.

Switch the needle or zipper foot to the opposite side to finish the second side of the zipper.

tip   *If you turn the zipper pull up toward the waistline edge, you will have an easier time sewing straight near the waistline.*

per foot, turning the work, then sewing along the side of the zipper, making sure you backstitch at the beginning and end of your sewing.

8. When you are finished stitching, press the zipper on the right side and on the wrong side. Remove the basting from the seam allowance, open the zipper, and press again. (See "Zipper Hints" on the facing page.)

LAPPED ZIPPERS Lapped zippers are characterized by a single row of topstitching along one side of the zipper. They are more complicated to construct than centered zippers, but this construction technique is one every sewer should have in her or his bag of tricks.

1. As with a centered zipper, prepare the garment by sewing the ⅝-in. seam allowance with a basting stitch in the zipper area, stopping and pulling the work out of the machine to leave a thread tail. Finish sewing the rest of the ⅝-in. seam with a regular stitch length, backstitching

tip   *Check your work from the right side of the garment. Are the stitching lines straight and an even distant from the seamline? If not, fix the problem now. It's easy to go back and fix an inch or two of uneven stitches.*

at the beginning and end of the line of stitches to lock the stitches.

2. Press the seam allowances open and press the zipper flat.

3. Lay the garment on a flat surface, wrong side up, with the waistline edge closest to you, then lay the zipper right side down, centering the zipper teeth along the seamline. (This is the way a packaged zipper is illustrated; I'm just annotating those instructions.)

4. Pin the right side of the zipper tape to the right side seam allowance only, pinning along the center of the tape, which may be indicated by a pulled thread or a change in weave. This is the right side as you are looking at it, with the garment wrong side up and top side down.

5. Before you sew, change the all-purpose presser foot on your sewing machine to the zipper foot, and position it so that the needle is on the left side of the foot. Using a long basting stitch (4 to 6 stitches per inch), sew the zipper tape to the seam allowance only (see the left photo on p. 62).

6. Take the garment out of the machine, and flip the zipper so it is right side up. The garment should be on the left and the unattached side of the zipper on the right.

7. Reposition the needle so it is again between the zipper teeth and the foot. Using a regular stitch length, sew a line of stitching to the right of the seamline and parallel to the zipper teeth through all the layers that are folded back (see the right photo on p. 62).

8. With the garment positioned wrong side up, flip the zipper right side down, lining up the zipper teeth as much as possible with the

Here are some hints to help you when inserting zippers.

Hint No. 1: Position the zipper stop at the end mark for the zipper, letting a too-long zipper hang over the waistline edge. Be sure to leave the too-long ends in place until the waistband is added. If you cut off the ends before adding the waistband and closing the zipper, the zipper pull will come off the tape, you won't be able to open the zipper, and you will have to take out the zipper and start all over again.

Hint No. 2: If you are fussy about how your garments look (like many home sewers of the world), you will want to hand-baste the zipper in place after you pin and before you sew. Using a needle with double thread, make a row of running stitches next to your line of pins, keeping the stitches even and not too big. The basting line will be your sewing guideline rather than the pin line. The work is flatter after you've removed the pins, the basting prevents the zipper from shifting, and it's easier to concentrate on sewing a straight line when sewing on the right side of the garment.

Hint No. 3: Topstitch a centered or lapped zipper, which means sewing on the top—the right side—of the garment. While many of the newer sewing machines have stitches that look as good on one side as on the other, you can see how the stitches look and if the line is straight when you sew on the top. Sometimes perfectly even stitching on one side of the fabric doesn't look equally perfect on the other side.

Hint No. 4: Although zippers can have metal or plastic teeth, the zipper tape is a pretty standard weight, often in contrast to the lighter-weight fabrics I like to use for gar-ment construction. To prevent the garment seam allowances from becoming wavy where the zipper has been inserted, interface them. After basting the seam allowance and sewing the remaining seam, place $1/2$-in.-wide strips of fusible interfacing that are as long as the zipper on the wrong side of the seam allowances (see the photo below). The interfacing will be behind the zipper and will beef up the seam allowances so that they are compatible with the weight of the zipper tape.

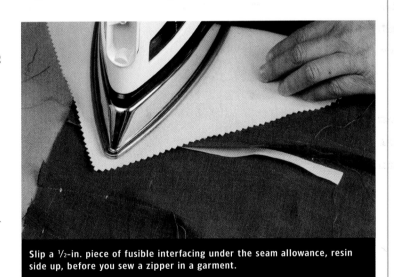

Slip a $1/2$-in. piece of fusible interfacing under the seam allowance, resin side up, before you sew a zipper in a garment.

seamline. There should be a small pleat at the bottom of the zipper. Pin the unattached side of the zipper in place through all thicknesses.

9. Turn the work over and repin on the right side of the garment, removing the pins on the wrong side. Be careful to keep the zipper in position when you flip the pins to the right side, and try to pin down the middle of the zipper tape. Next, hand-baste along the line of pins to secure the zipper (see the photo on p. 63). This will eliminate the need for pins and create a thread guideline for sewing.

10. Before you sew, move the needle or the zipper foot so that the needle is closer to the

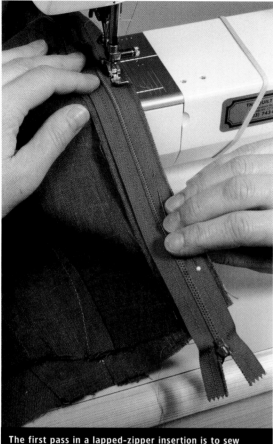

The first pass in a lapped-zipper insertion is to sew the left side of the zipper tape to the left seam allowance only.

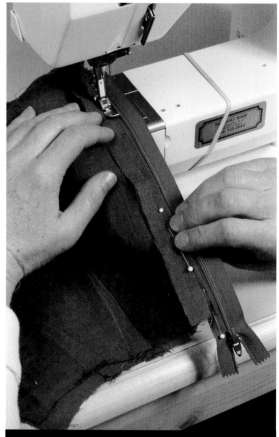

On the second pass, flip the zipper so that it is right side up (check the zipper pull if you are not sure) and sew through all layers right next to the zipper teeth.

zipper teeth than the zipper foot is. Position the garment in the sewing machine with the needle at the bottom of the zipper at the seam. Sewing through all thicknesses, sew across the bottom of the zipper until you are in line with the pins or your basted line, stopping with the needle down in the garment. Lift the zipper foot and turn the work, lower the foot, and continue sewing parallel to the seam to the waistline edge of the garment. Backstitch at the beginning and end of your stitching (see the illustration on the facing page). I always follow Zipper Hint No. 2, given in "Zipper

Hints" on p. 61, when making a lapped zipper, basting before topstitching the zipper in place through all layers of fabric.

11. When you are finished stitching, press the right side and the wrong side of the zipper. Remove the basting from the seam allowance and open the zipper.

INVISIBLE ZIPPERS When you look at a garment that has an invisible zipper, you'll see only the zipper pull at the top of the closed zipper. There is no topstitching at all on the garment. This zipper is not difficult to insert once you

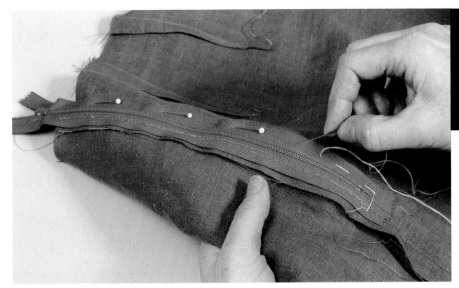

Before finishing the zipper by stitching on the right side of the garment, hand-baste the zipper in place. The zipper won't shift around, and the basting will give you a guideline to follow.

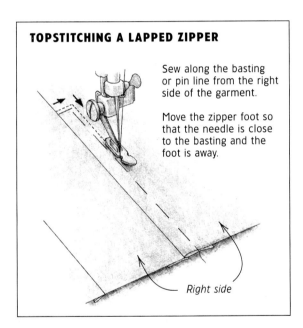

TOPSTITCHING A LAPPED ZIPPER

Sew along the basting or pin line from the right side of the garment.

Move the zipper foot so that the needle is close to the basting and the foot is away.

Right side

have figured out where you are sewing each step of the way.

1. An invisible zipper is much like a regular zipper except the line of teeth is somewhat coiled on an invisible zipper. Begin by opening the zipper and pressing the teeth as flat as you can (see the left photo on p. 64).

2. Since the seam is not sewn before the zipper is inserted in this zipper application, fold to the wrong side and press the standard ⅝-in. seam allowances in the garment where the zipper will be.

3. Looking at the wrong side of the garment pieces, align the pressed-back seam allowances. Open the zipper and lay it face down on the seam allowances, then match and pin each side of the zipper tape to each seam allowance. A single pin in each side is all you need to get yourself oriented.

4. Working on the seam allowance on the right, pin the zipper tape to the seam allowance along the entire length of the zipper opening, aligning the zipper teeth to the folded edge of the seam allowance (see the right photo on p. 64). Make sure you pin only the zipper tape to the seam allowance—do not catch any of the garment.

5. Before you sew, change the all-purpose presser foot on your sewing machine to the

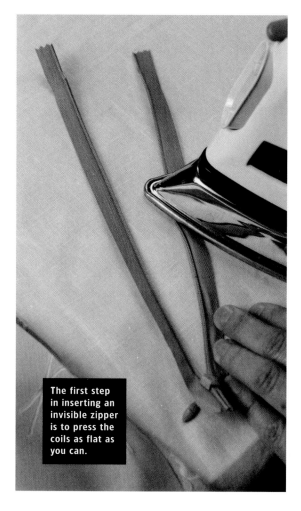

The first step in inserting an invisible zipper is to press the coils as flat as you can.

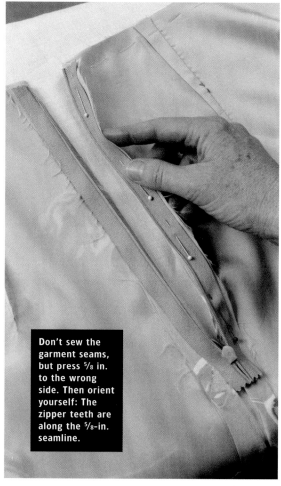

Don't sew the garment seams, but press ⅝ in. to the wrong side. Then orient yourself: The zipper teeth are along the ⅝-in. seamline.

zipper foot, and move the needle so that it is between the zipper teeth and the foot. Sew the zipper tape to the seam allowance as far down as you can (see the top photo on the facing page). It will not be possible to sew past the zipper pull at the bottom of the open zipper.

6. After finishing the first side, reposition the garment as it was when your started: The wrong side of the garment is up, the pressed-back seam allowances are side by side, and the zipper is face down. Pin the left side of the open zipper to the left seam allowance, aligning the zipper teeth to the folded edge of the

seam allowance (see the bottom photo on the facing page). Sew the zipper tape to the seam allowance only, sewing as far down as you can.

7. To finish the bottom of the zipper, close it and place the two garment pieces with the zipper attached right sides together. Flatten the pieces where the zipper is attached as much as possible, and pin, starting where the zipper attachment stitches stop and going all the way to the hem. Because it's important that the seam below the zipper doesn't come undone after the garment is finished, stabilize this area

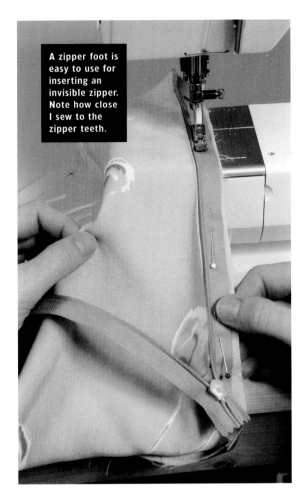

A zipper foot is easy to use for inserting an invisible zipper. Note how close I sew to the zipper teeth.

by pinning a small square of stay tape at the beginning of the stitch line.

Because of the zipper stop, it's not possible to have a continuous line of stitching from the zipper to the hem, but it's not important that there is one. Once again using a zipper foot on the machine, position the needle so that it is between the foot and the zipper teeth. Sew from the bottom of the zipper opening to the end of the seam, backstitching at the beginning and end of the stitching line (see the photo on p. 66). Be careful to sew the seam below the zipper at ⅝ in.

Constructing waistbands

Two types of waistband construction are included here. The first is the classic-fitted waistband and the second is the contour waist-

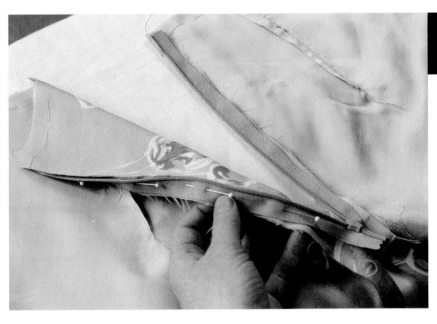

Reorient yourself for the second pass. The teeth are along the seamline of the second side.

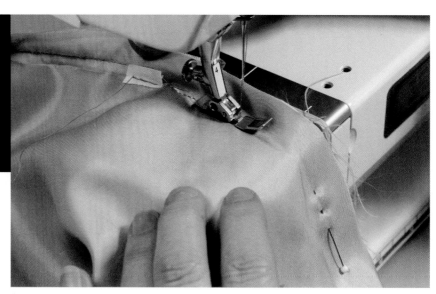

To finish the zipper, zip it up and hold the seam allowances together as much as you can. Stitch, sewing a small piece of stay tape at the bottom of the zipper. You will finish the seam allowance with the zipper foot on the machine, so be careful that you know where your ⁵⁄₈-in. seam allowance is.

band. Both are commonly found in ready-to-wear garments.

CLASSIC-FITTED WAISTBAND A classic-fitted waistband is typically 1 in. to 2 in. wide and sits above the waistline edge of the skirt or pants. The pattern piece is a long rectangle, which is cut on the straight grain of the fabric. Men's pants traditionally have a waistband with a seam in the center back, a construction seen from time to time in ladies' clothing as well.

Constructing a fitted waistband requires the use of some type of interfacing or stiffening material. At the zipper opening, the waistband can have an overlap, which is an extension that is visible on the right side of the garment, or an underlap, if the extension is hidden by the waistband.

1. Begin by looking at the pattern piece. Typically, there are many markings: center back, center front, notches, pairs of dots (gen-

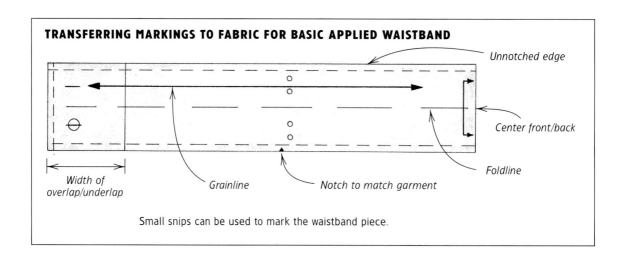

TRANSFERRING MARKINGS TO FABRIC FOR BASIC APPLIED WAISTBAND

Unnotched edge

Center front/back

Foldline

Width of overlap/underlap

Grainline

Notch to match garment

Small snips can be used to mark the waistband piece.

Interfacing is a type of material that supports and stabilizes the fashion fabric pieces used in garment construction. Used extensively in jacket making, interfacing has many applications in less-constructed garments. It helps shape pieces like collars and cuffs, it supports buttonholes and buttons, it prevents pockets from sagging out of shape, and it keeps waistbands upright and crisp. There are two broad types of interfacing: sew-in and iron-on, also called fusible. Each type is available in a variety of weights and in a few colors.

Interfacing should be used in waistbands, since all waistbands need some stiffening to keep them from collapsing. The types of interfacing you can use for waistbands include sew-in and fusible packaged waistband material that keeps bulk out of the folded part of the waistband—stiff waistbanding sold by the yard and used in a single layer in the waistband, and sew-in and fusible interfacing sold by the yard and cut to match the pattern piece.

If you are using sew-in or fusible interfacing that is cut from the pattern piece or packaged interfacing material, apply it to the waistband before attaching the waistband to the garment. Apply sew-in interfacing by hand-basting it to the wrong side of the fabric waistband piece, sewing 1/2 in. from the edges.

If you are using fusible interfacing, place the waistband wrong side up on an ironing board and place the interfacing wrong side down on the waistband. The wrong side of the interfacing is the side with the glue, or resin, which is sometimes bumpy. (If you are not sure which is the glue side, test a piece between two pieces of scrap fabric.) Place a press cloth on top of the interfacing and spritz with water. Using an iron on a hot setting, press the interfacing to the fabric in sections, holding the iron 10 seconds on each section.

erally indicating matchpoints for side seams), button and buttonhole markings, overlap or underlap, foldline, and sometimes grainline. The important markings to transfer to the fabric are the notches that match the garment, the center front or center back, and the width of the overlap/underlap (see the illustration on the facing page).

2. Select an interfacing for the waistband. (See "Adding Interfacing to Waistbands" above.) If you are using a sew-in or fusible interfacing, attach it to the waistband now; if you are using stiff waistbanding, add it after the waistband is sewn to the garment.

3. With right sides together, match and pin the notched edge of the waistband to the waistline edge of the garment, matching the center front (or center back) and any notches, and allowing

tip *When applying fusible interfacing, it is important to use a press cloth just in case the interfacing is glue side up. A press cloth prevents the interfacing from sticking to your iron and also dissipates the heat over the interfacing, which needs the heat from the hot iron to set the resin but would melt if touched by the iron.*

the overlap/underlap to extend beyond one end of the waistband. Stitch, using a 5/8-in. seam allowance (see the photo on p. 68).

4. If you are using stiff waistbanding, attach it to the waistband now. Place the material on top of both seam allowances along the seam

STAYSTITCH-PLUS

Staystitch-plus is an important technique to learn. The technique is used for shaping the curved edge of an easy patch pocket, for setting jacket sleeves, and for matching two layers that need to match but don't.

To use staystitch-plus, press your finger behind the presser foot of your machine while you sew a row of stitches through a single layer of fabric. Your finger will work as a dam, preventing the fabric from flowing freely under the foot. The fabric will crimp up. When the fabric stops moving at all, release your finger and start again. Don't smooth out the fabric behind the presser foot, since that would take away the effect you are looking for. You should be able to ease the garment in several inches using this technique.

If you have trouble getting the fabric to crimp up behind the presser foot, try pushing the fabric in from the front while keeping your finger firmly in place behind the foot.

You can add ease by making parallel rows of staystitch-plus—even stitching on top of the stitches. Just keep all the stitching inside the ⅝-in. seam allowance so none will show on the finished garment.

Attach the waistband to the waistline edge of the garment with right sides together. The seam allowance and the underlap/overlap will extend beyond the edge.

tip *The garment waistline may have stretched or relaxed a bit since you cut it out. If it does not match the waistband, make the waistband smaller by easing the unfinished edge using the technique known as staystitch-plus (see "Staystitch-Plus" above).*

you have just sewn, making sure the material matches the entire length of the waistband including seam allowances and overlap/underlap. Stitch it in place using a long zigzag stitch (see the left photo on the facing page).

5. Press the waistband and both seam allowances up above the garment.

6. Trim ⅜ in. from the unnotched edge of the waistband, making sure you don't cut off more because you'll need ¼ in. to anchor the waistband. Finish the unnotched edge with one of

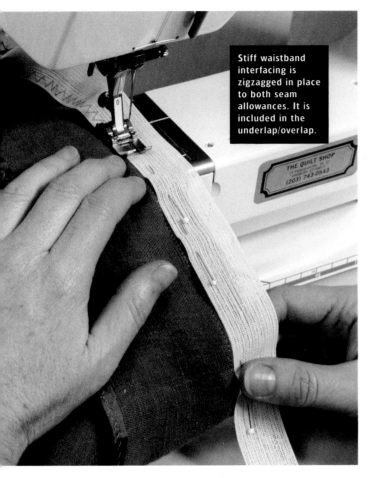

Stiff waistband interfacing is zigzagged in place to both seam allowances. It is included in the underlap/overlap.

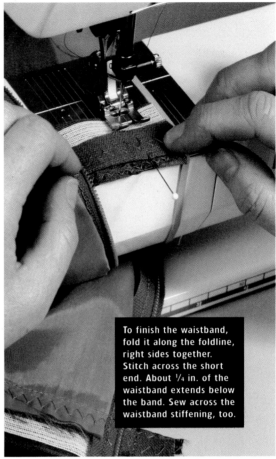

To finish the waistband, fold it along the foldline, right sides together. Stitch across the short end. About ¼ in. of the waistband extends below the band. Sew across the waistband stiffening, too.

the seam finishes described in "Finishing Unsewn Edges" on p. 38.

7. Next, with right sides together, fold the waistband along the foldline. Using a ⅝ in. seam allowance, sew across each short end of the waistband through all thicknesses of fabric, seam allowances, and interfacing (see the right photo above). Trim the ends close to the stitching line, then turn the band right side out. Press the waistband along the foldline.

8. To finish the waistband, pin so that the ¼-in. finished edge is just below the attachment seam. Pin from the right side of the garment through all thicknesses. In the overlap/underlap area, tuck the finished edge up into the waistband and above the zipper. Stitch in the ditch along the seamline (see "Stitch in the Ditch" on p. 44), using your fingers to keep the ditch visible and checking with your thumb that the underside of where you are sewing is flat with nothing caught (see the photo on p. 70). Lastly, topstitch the tuck-in finished edge along the overlap/underlap.

CONTOUR WAISTBAND A garment with a contour waistline doesn't have a band that sits above the waist. Instead, the top of the garment is finished on the inside with a piece that is the same shape as the top of the garment but is

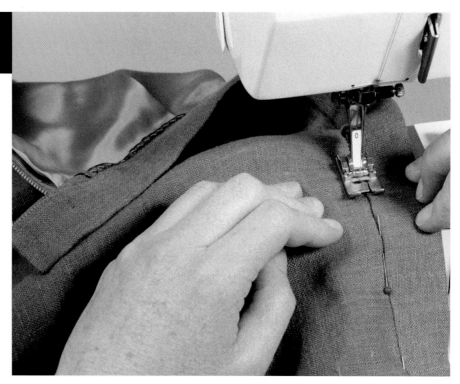

Stitch in the ditch from the right side of the garment to anchor the waistband.

only about 3 in. wide. This piece, which is the facing, will often have all the same fitting details as the garment itself, such as darts, although the darts may not be as long as they are on the garment.

1. Begin by cutting and marking the garment pieces. For the facing, cut the pieces from fabric and interfacing, then attach the interfacing to the fabric (see "Adding Interfacing to Waistbands" on p. 67 and the photo on the facing page).

2. Just as on the garment, transfer the markings for the darts to the interfaced facing pieces. The other markings that are important to transfer to the fabric are the notches on the waistline edge. These are the points that will match up with the garment waistline edge.

3. Sew the darts, then press them toward the center of the facing pieces.

4. Next, sew the facing pieces together along any seams to create one long facing piece.

5. Finish the unnotched edge of the facing, using a zigzag or overlock stitch or a type of binding. Since the zipper should already be inserted in the garment, trim ⅝ in. from each short end before finishing or fold in ⅝ in. and press.

6. Before attaching the facing to the garment, add stay tape to the waistline to prevent it from stretching while you are wearing the garment. Begin by cutting a piece of stay tape the same length as your waist. (See "Stay Tape" on p. 56.) Mark the center of the tape with a pencil or marking pen, then, on the wrong side of the garment, place the stay tape ⅝ in. from the waistline edge, matching the center front with the mark on the center of the tape. Pin at the center, each end, and between the

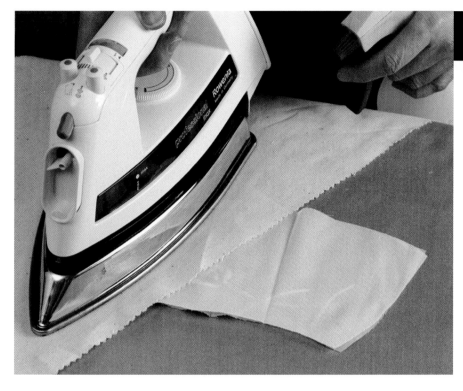

ends. The tape may just fit or it may seem a bit small for the garment, which means the garment has already stretched out of shape. With the tape side up, sew the tape in place, stitch-

tip *Whenever you are sewing a shorter piece of fabric to a longer one, sew with the short piece up. In the case of a contoured waistband, the waistline stay is shorter than the garment. The feed dogs on the sewing machine will take up more of the bottom piece than the top, thereby easing it, and matching it, to what's on top.*

ing a little less than ⅝ in. from the waistline edge.

7. Next, attach the facing to the garment, which at this point has its darts constructed, zipper inserted, side seams sewn, and waistline stayed. With right sides together, match and pin the facing to the waistline edge of the garment. Stitch ⅝ in. from the edge, backstitching at the beginning and the end of the line of stitches (see the top photo on p. 72).

8. Press the facing and both seam allowances above the garment, then understitch the facing. To understitch, sew both seam allowances to the facing ⅛ in. from the seamline, taking care to keep the facing smooth and flat.

9. Trim, grading the seam allowances (see the bottom photo on p. 72). Grading is a method of

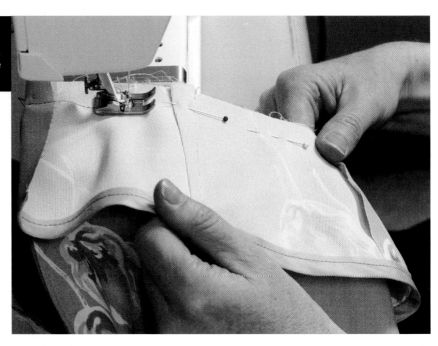

Turn in and press the seam allowance on the short end of the facing. With right sides together, match and sew the facing to the garment.

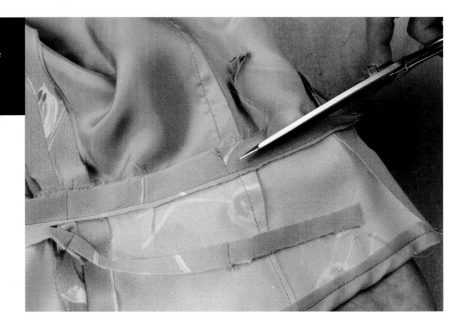

Eliminate bulky seams by grading them as you trim. The seam allowance closest to the facing is cut more than the seam allowance closest to the garment.

trimming used to eliminate bulk. With this technique, the seam allowances are cut to graduated widths, one narrower than the other. If you flip the facing into its finished position, you will notice that both seam allowances are right next to each other. Check out which of these seam allowances is next to the top side of the garment. This seam allowance should be trimmed a bit (about ¼ in.), but the second seam allowance should be trimmed a lot (about ⅜ in).

10. Hand-stitch the short end of the facing in place along the zipper tape. Add a hook and eye or thread loop above the zipper in the gap between the top of the zipper and the waistline edge.

Hemming by hand

Before hemming a garment, try it on to determine the correct length for you. Fold excess fabric to the wrong side of the garment and pin in place, then take the garment off and lay it on a flat surface. Line up the front and back along the waistline seam. Measure the hem you have pinned, then pin the hem evenly all around the garment.

Hems can vary in depth, but having a hem that is too deep weights the bottom of a garment and can distort the shape. If you have folded up more than 2 in. of fabric, cut off the excess, taking care to leave an even 1½-in. to 2-in. hem all the way around. Measure with a small seam guide, and pin or mark with chalk before you cut.

If the fabric ravels easily, it may be necessary to finish the hem edge using rayon seam tape or a Hong Kong finish (see p. 38). With some lightweight fabrics, you can simply fold the top of the hem under ½ in.

Try on the garment one more time after you have pinned the hem to make sure you've got it right. Next, choose a hand-stitching needle that is appropriate for your fabric—one that is sharp so that it doesn't leave holes but one with a large enough eye for your thread. Generally, the finer the thread you are using, the smaller the needle, and the finer the fabric you are using, the finer the thread. When choosing thread for hems, I like to use silk thread since it blends into the fabric. If you don't have silk thread, use the thread you constructed the garment with.

Once you've chosen your needle and thread, thread the needle with a single thread and knot it. Don't put too much thread on the needle or it's sure to tangle. Sit in a well-lit place, then, working on the wrong side of the garment, begin sewing using one of the following three stitches: the fell stitch, blindstitch, and blind catchstitch. These are interchangeable and are all good stitches to have in your repertoire.

FELL STITCH Most hand-stitching works from right to left, in this case with the hem below the needle. To hem using a fell stitch, start by putting the needle in the fabric on the hem edge and hiding the knot on the wrong side of the hem. The stitches are worked right along the top of the hem. Make the stitch by putting the needle in on the hem side and out on the garment side, catching only a few threads of the garment before pulling the thread out (see the top illustration on p. 74).

BLINDSTITCH A second type of stitch used for hemming is the blindstitch. Again, working from right to left with the hem below the needle, start by putting the needle in the fabric on the hem edge and hiding the knot on the wrong side of the hem. The stitches are worked back and forth between the hem and the garment along the top edge of the hem. Take a small stitch on the hem side, then take a small stitch on the garment side, catching only a few threads of the garment. The second stitch

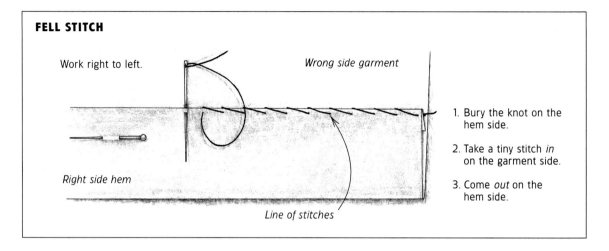

FELL STITCH

Work right to left.

Wrong side garment

Right side hem

Line of stitches

1. Bury the knot on the hem side.

2. Take a tiny stitch *in* on the garment side.

3. Come *out* on the hem side.

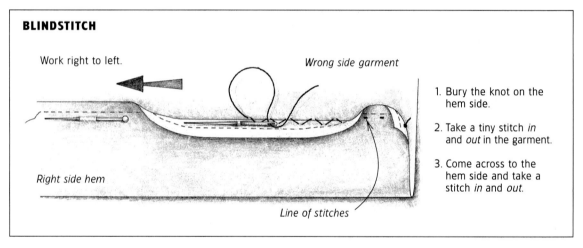

BLINDSTITCH

Work right to left.

Wrong side garment

Right side hem

Line of stitches

1. Bury the knot on the hem side.

2. Take a tiny stitch *in* and *out* in the garment.

3. Come across to the hem side and take a stitch *in* and *out*.

comes back to the hem side, where a small stitch is taken, then it's back to the garment for a small stitch, catching only a few garment threads (see the bottom illustration above). Continue in this manner.

BLIND CATCHSTITCH The blind catchstitch works from left to right. Just as with the blindstitch, the stitches are worked back and forth between the hem and the garment along the top edge of the hem. Starting on the left with the hem below the needle, put the needle in the fabric on the hem side, hiding the knot on the wrong side of the hem. Draw the thread across to the garment side and take a small stitch, placing the needle in on the right and out on the left, catching only a few garment threads. The second stitch is taken on the hem side by taking a small stitch in on the right and out on the left, pulling the needle out and over the thread on the left (see the top illustration on the facing page). Moving to the right, the third stitch is taken on the garment side, with the needle in on the right side and pulled out and over the thread on the left. Because the

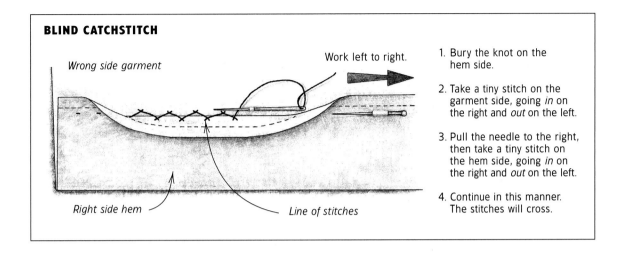

BLIND CATCHSTITCH

Wrong side garment

Work left to right.

Right side hem

Line of stitches

1. Bury the knot on the hem side.

2. Take a tiny stitch on the garment side, going *in* on the right and *out* on the left.

3. Pull the needle to the right, then take a tiny stitch on the hem side, going *in* on the right and *out* on the left.

4. Continue in this manner. The stitches will cross.

stitches are worked left to right but the stitches are made right to left, they will crisscross.

Advanced hemming

Once you have mastered the basic hand-hemming techniques, you may want to try more advanced ones, such as mitering and sewing curved hems.

MITERING Mitering is a great finish for a slit in a straight skirt. The iron does most of the work in this construction technique.

1. Begin by folding and pressing two adjacent edges to the wrong side by an equal amount (see the illustration at right). For example, on a skirt with a slit, press the hem up 1 in., and press the edges that will form the slit in 1 in. Unfold the two edges.

2. On the right side, the lines made by pressing form a square where they cross at the corner. Fold the corner in toward the skirt on the diagonal, so that the visible pressing lines match. Press again so that there is a long diagonal press (see the left illustrations on p. 76). Unfold the diagonal.

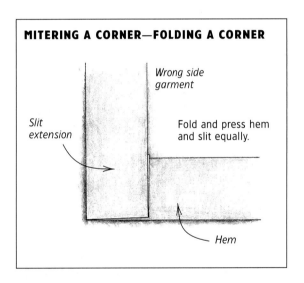

MITERING A CORNER—FOLDING A CORNER

Slit extension

Wrong side garment

Fold and press hem and slit equally.

Hem

3. Next, with right sides together, fold the corner in half diagonally. The diagonal press lines will be back-to-back and matching. Pin, then sew from the outside edge toward the folded edge along the diagonal foldline, using a regular stitch length until you are about ½ in. from the folded edge. Then shorten the stitch length and continue sewing to the folded edge (see the right illustration on p. 76).

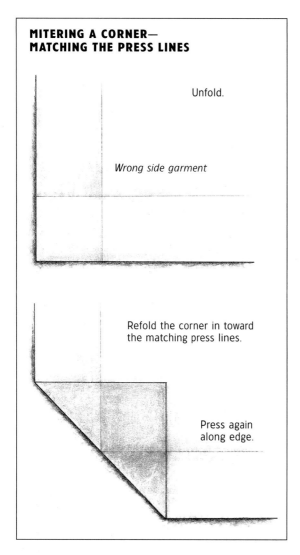

Unfold.

Wrong side garment

Refold the corner in toward
the matching press lines.

Press again
along edge.

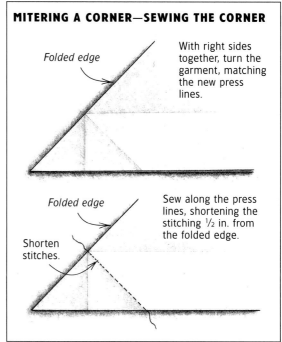

Folded edge

With right sides
together, turn the
garment, matching
the new press
lines.

Folded edge

Sew along the press
lines, shortening the
stitching ½ in. from
the folded edge.

Shorten
stitches.

The trick you can use to easily hem a curved edge is staystitch-plus (see the sidebar on p. 68). Without staystitch-plus, you would have little gathers and puckers or little tucks in the hem to make it lay flat against the garment. And, frankly, hems like that often look terrible—bulky, likely to show on the right side of the garment, and really homemade.

4. Trim the corner close to the stitching line. Turn the garment right side out and press (see the illustration on the facing page).

CURVED HEMS Hemming a garment with distinctive curve, such as a tulip skirt, a circle skirt, or an A-line skirt, can be difficult because a larger circle is turned up and stitched against a smaller circle. (I was terrible in geometry in high school, and it is coming back to haunt me!)

1. To make a curved hem, measure and pin the hem to the desired length. Trim the folded-back fabric so that the hem is narrow, about 1 in. to 1½ in. If the fabric tends to ravel, finish the hem edge.

2. Staystitch-plus all the way around the garment ½ in. from the cut edge of the hem. Because the hem is narrow and you are not trying to match dramatically disparate curves, you can use light pressure when placing your

MITERING A CORNER—FINISHING

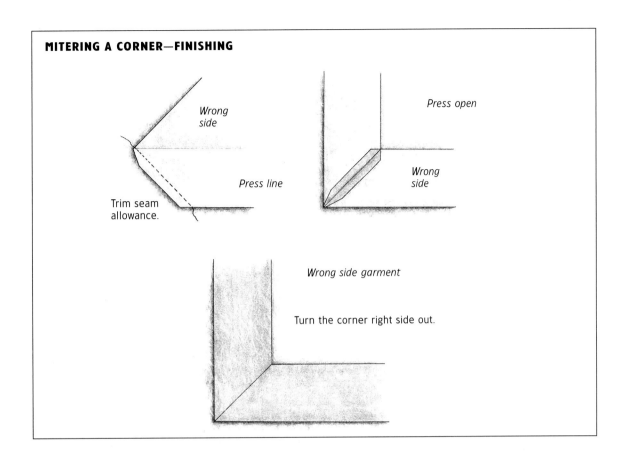

Wrong side

Press line

Trim seam allowance.

Press open

Wrong side

Wrong side garment

Turn the corner right side out.

finger behind the presser foot. Remember not to smooth out the fabric behind the presser foot, since that would take away the effect you are creating.

3. After using staystitch–plus, press the hem into place on the wrong side of the garment. It

tip *If you have crimped up too much fabric when using staystitch-plus and the hem is actually smaller than the edge you need to match, pop a few threads to relax the fabric. If the hem is still too big and you are tempted to pleat the fabric, go back and staystitch-plus some more.*

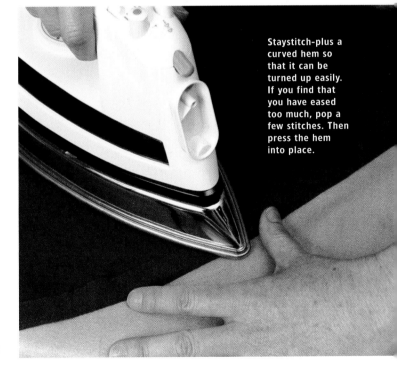

Staystitch-plus a curved hem so that it can be turned up easily. If you find that you have eased too much, pop a few stitches. Then press the hem into place.

should lie flat, ready for you to pin and sew by machine or by hand (see the photo on p. 77).

Attaching hooks and eyes and snaps

Hooks and eyes and snaps are best attached to a garment with a needle that has been threaded with a double thread. If you wish, draw double thread over a piece of beeswax to strengthen it.

After figuring out where the hook or snap needs to go, pin or tape it in place until you get started. Begin sewing by hiding the knot under the snap or between the attachment loops on the hook, then take even stitches. Make sure your stitches don't show on the other side of

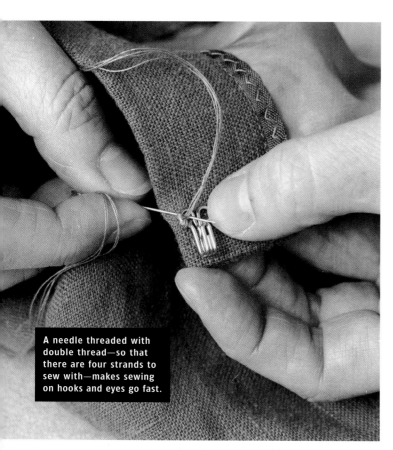

A needle threaded with double thread—so that there are four strands to sew with—makes sewing on hooks and eyes go fast.

> **tip** *Thread can be strengthened by running it over a piece of beeswax. Beeswax is available in a little cake, much like a tiny bar of soap. Lay the thread on the beeswax, then pull the thread across the surface while holding it with your thumb to lightly coat it with the wax.*

the fabric by placing the fingers of your non-dominant hand under the hook or snap (see the photo below).

An alternate to using an eye is to use a thread loop. To make a thread loop, begin by threading a needle with a double thread that is long enough to complete the entire loop. This is probably the only time I recommend having a long length of thread on a needle. Knot the thread and hide the knot on the wrong side of the garment. Next, make the bar by pulling the needle out at the bottom of the loop and anchoring the loop at the top end by taking a tiny stitch above where you started. The bar needs to be long enough for the button or hook but not too long or too tight against the fabric. Finish the bar by anchoring it with a tiny stitch right where you started. Because you are working with four threads, there will now be a bar of eight threads (see the left illustration on the facing page).

Next, cover the bar with stitches by making a loop of thread on the left of the bar, then bringing the needle under the bar and over the loop. Pull the thread to tighten each stitch

MAKING A THREAD BAR

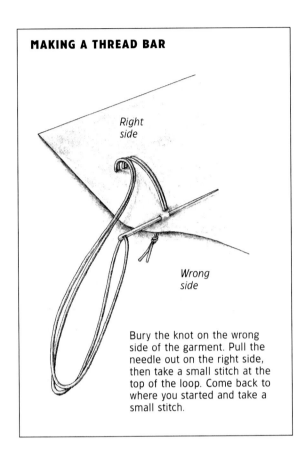

Right side

Wrong side

Bury the knot on the wrong side of the garment. Pull the needle out on the right side, then take a small stitch at the top of the loop. Come back to where you started and take a small stitch.

FORMING THE STITCH

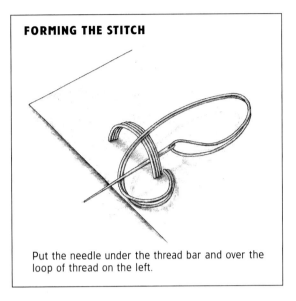

Put the needle under the thread bar and over the loop of thread on the left.

KEEPING THE STITCHES EVEN

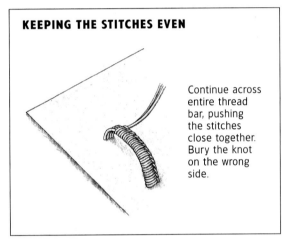

Continue across entire thread bar, pushing the stitches close together. Bury the knot on the wrong side.

around the bar, and use your fingernails to lay the stitches in place side by side. The stitches will start to twist, much like macrame half-hitches do, which will be most noticeable if the thread loop is long. Try to keep the stitches next to each other, ignoring the twist. When you get to the top of the bar, pull the needle through to the wrong side of the garment and knot the thread (see the illustrations at right).

Creating belt loops

I like the unobtrusiveness of a thread loop for a belt, but sometimes the belt for a skirt of robe needs a more substantial holder. In these cases, I make belt loops from fabric that matches the garment.

FINISHING THE THREAD LOOP

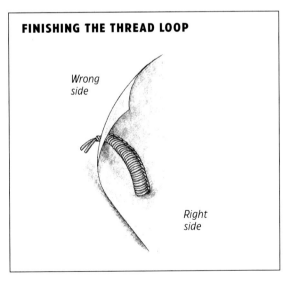

Wrong side

Right side

ATTACHING THE FLY EXTENSION

Place the fly extension along the edge of the right extension. Pin and stitch the fly extension to the right extension only, then stitch across the curve to further anchor the fly extension.

11. To finish the project, turn the garment to the right side. Make a small satin stitch where the topstitching meets the seamline at the bottom of the zipper. A satin stitch is a very short zigzag stitch (14 to 16 stitches per inch or 0.5 mm). The width of the zigzag can vary from 3 to 5 stitches per inch. Make about 6 stitches.

Adding a lining

A lining is added to a garment before the waistband or waistline facing is attached. I like slippery linings and always line simple skirts so

toward the long folded side. Trim excess fabric from the curve, then turn the piece right side out. Press the fly extension flat and straight stitch, zigzag, or serge the unfolded edges together.

10. On the wrong side of the garment, position and pin the unfolded edge of the fly extension along the right side of the zipper extension so that the curved end is toward the zipper stop. Sew in place, making sure you attach the fly extension and zipper extension only (see the illustration above). To further anchor the fly extension, sew the curved edge to the left zipper extension.

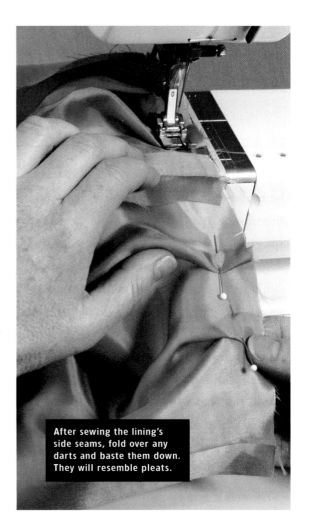

After sewing the lining's side seams, fold over any darts and baste them down. They will resemble pleats.

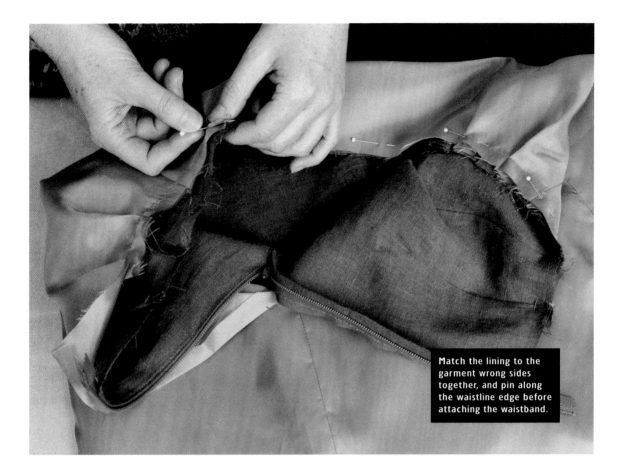

Match the lining to the garment wrong sides together, and pin along the waistline edge before attaching the waistband.

I never need to wear a slip. Whether you are lining a skirt or a pair of pants, begin by cutting a second set of garment pieces, except the waistband, in lightweight fabric such as Bemberg rayon.

The lining seams are sewn just as the seams of the garment are. However, darts in the lining are not sewn, but rather are simply pleated out at the waistline edge and basted down (see the photo on the facing page). Press open the lining's seam allowances and leave the zipper area open with seam allowances pressed back.

Before attaching the waistband, place and pin the wrong side of the lining against the wrong side of the garment (see the photo above). Baste along the waistline edge by hand or with long machine stitches. Complete the garment construction by adding the waistband or facing.

To finish the garment, hand-stitch the pressed-back seam allowances of the lining along both sides of the zipper tape. Hem the lining so that it is shorter than the garment (you can stitch the lining hem by machine).

easy tops, dresses, and vests

■ ■ 3 ■

T-shirt tops, easy dresses, and vests are fun to make. Lots of simple garments can be made with minimal sewing skills. It is often fabulous fabric that disguises how simple these wardrobe pieces are to construct.

Pull-on pants
Pattern: Textile
Studio Pant 1001
Fabric: Cotton/linen
Needle: 80/12 H
Thread: Mettler
silk-finish cotton
Straight stitch, 2.5

Vest
Pattern: Butterick
6497
Fabric: 100% cotton
Needle: 80/12 H
Thread: Mettler
silk-finish cotton
Straight stitch, 2.5

■ T-SHIRT TOPS AND DRESSES

Easy tops include simple dresses as well as T-shirts because the basic construction techniques are the same—dresses are just longer versions of T-shirts. For a first project or a fast one, choose fabric from the list on pp. 4-5. When you are ready to challenge yourself, make these same basic garments in more luxurious fabric, using the same techniques.

Marking the fabric

After you have cut out the garment pieces, look for markings you need to transfer to the fabric. Look for the notches, which are the small triangles on the edges of the pattern pieces, and any dots, which are matchpoints typically inside the edges of the pattern. I recommend you transfer the notches from the pattern pieces to the fabric with small, ⅛-in. snips. Use tailor tacks, chalk, or marking pens to transfer dots, triangles, and squares from the pattern to the fabric.

> ### CONSTRUCTING EASY TOPS AND DRESSES
>
> • Cut out the fabric pieces.
> • Transfer all markings from the pattern to the fabric.
> • Sew darts or princess seams.
> • Sew shoulder seams.
> • Sew easy sleeves.
> • Sew side seams.
> • Finish the neck and armhole edges.
> • Hem the garment.

After completing all the marking, take the pattern pieces off the fabric. If you can't tell the right side of the fabric from the wrong side, either mark the wrong side with peel-and-stick labels or make an X in chalk. Repin the pattern pieces to the fabric pieces until you are ready to use them.

Sewing darts

Darts are fitting elements that are found in skirts, slacks, blouses, dresses—almost any garment. They appear on pattern pieces as triangles, and when sewn, pinch out more fabric at one end than at the other. These fitting elements point to fuller parts of the body: In tops, darts point to the bust, while in skirts and pants, they point to the hips.

1. Begin constructing a dart by transferring the shape of the dart to the fabric. There are several methods for transferring these marks. Trace the dart onto the wrong side of the fabric by using a tracing wheel and paper; use tailor tacks; use chalk or marking pens; or use a combination of snips and tailor tacks or chalk/markers (see the top illustration on the facing page). I use this last method. I make tiny snips at the edge of the garment to indicate the outer edges of the dart, then I make tailor tacks at the dart point. If the dart is longer than 4 in., I also make tailor tacks at the midpoint of each side of the dart, marking any small dots that appear on the pattern.

2. To sew a dart, fold the fabric right sides together along an imaginary line through the center of the triangular dart. Match the snips at

MARKING DARTS

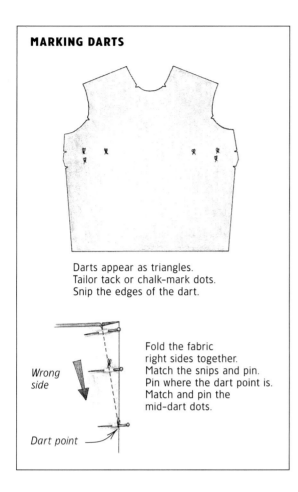

Darts appear as triangles.
Tailor tack or chalk-mark dots.
Snip the edges of the dart.

Wrong side

Fold the fabric
right sides together.
Match the snips and pin.
Pin where the dart point is.
Match and pin the
mid-dart dots.

Dart point

the edge and pin. Find the dart point and pin; this is where the stitching will end. Find any midpoint marks and pin these as well.

3. Next, imagine a straight line from the snips at the edge to the dart point. With chalk or pencil, lightly trace a line from the edge of the garment to the dart point: This is where you are going to sew. Using a regular stitch length, begin sewing at the edge, backstitching one or two stitches to lock them. When you are about ½ in. from the dart point, shorten your stitch length to 12 to 14 stitches per inch or 1.75 mm, and continue sewing. Sew off the fabric at the dart point without backstitching. The smaller stitches lock the threads, and there is no extra bulk at the dart point from backstitching.

If you are making a dress that has a double-pointed dart—one end that points up to the bust and one end that points down to the hip—divide the dart in two. Sew from the cen-

MARKING DOUBLE-POINTED DARTS

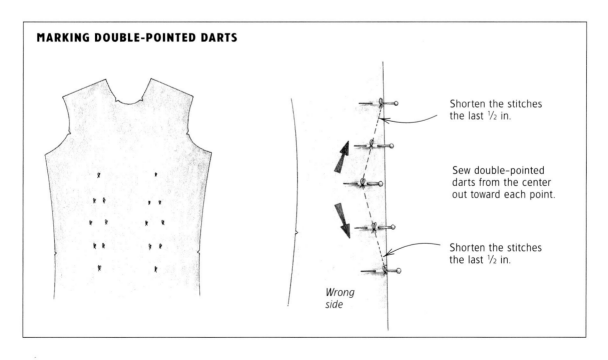

Shorten the stitches
the last ½ in.

Sew double-pointed
darts from the center
out toward each point.

Shorten the stitches
the last ½ in.

Wrong side

ter to one dart point, then from the center again to the second dart point. Remember to shorten the stitches about ½ in. from each dart point (see the illustration on p. 89).

4. Press bust darts down toward the waist. If you have constructed a double-pointed dart, press the dart toward the center of the garment.

Sewing pleats

Released pleats may appear in easy dresses instead of darts. Here they are similar to darts, but there are no dart points; the fabric is "released" at the fuller part of the figure. Released pleats help fit a garment to the body without being as fitted as a dart.

1. Mark released pleats as you would a dart without the dart points. Use tailor tacks, chalk, or other marking devices to mark the midpoints and end points.

2. Fold the garment along the imaginary foldline in the center of the pleat and pin, matching the midpoints and end points. Sew this line, starting and stopping at the end points and backstitching where you start and stop.

3. On the wrong side of the fabric, press the folded pleat toward the center of the garment.

Sewing princess seams

Princess seams are fitting elements that are easy to construct if you know how to and frustrating if you don't. The secret is staystitching. (See "Staystitching" below.)

Princess-seamed garments come in two shapes, one with a seam over the bustline from the shoulder to the hem, and the second with the seamline from a point on the armhole edge over the bust to the hem (see the illustration on the facing page). Since the seams curve, the pattern pieces are curved, but one curve is concave (a curve that goes in) and one is convex (a curve that goes out).

1. Begin constructing a princess seam by staystitching the concave curve. You need only staystitch the curved area, not the entire seam. After staystitching, clip to but not through the stitching line at intervals of ¾ in. to 1 in. along the curve (see the photo on the facing page).

STAYSTITCHING

Staystitching is stitching a regular-length stitch through one thickness of fabric just a bit closer to the cut edge of the fabric than the stitching line. When staystitching, sew $9/16$ in. from the edge rather than the typical $5/8$ in. Staystitching is often used for stabilizing neck edges, especially V-necks, and for princess seams, where staystitching allows you to clip close to the seamline without worry.

PRINCESS SEAMS

TWO STYLES

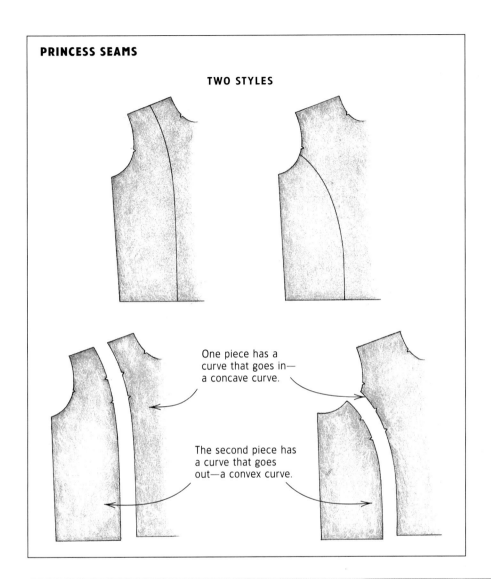

One piece has a curve that goes in—a concave curve.

The second piece has a curve that goes out—a convex curve.

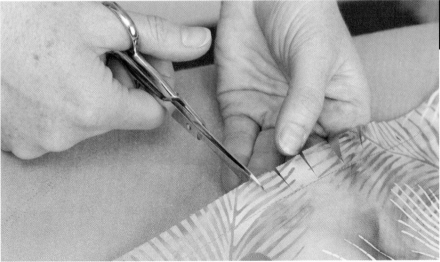

Staystitch then clip the concave curve of a princess seam.

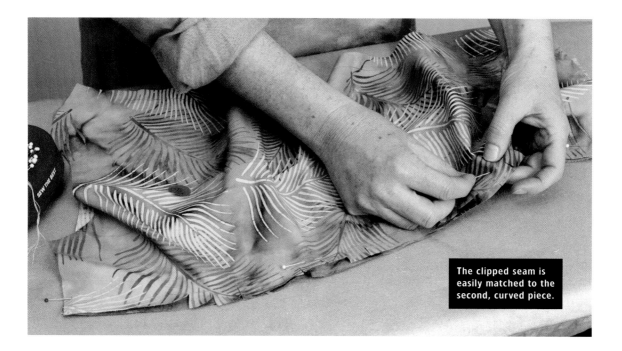

The clipped seam is easily matched to the second, curved piece.

Don't clip where the notch is, though, because you need this matchpoint to line up the second piece.

2. Next, with right sides together, match and pin the two curved pieces, first by matching the notch and the top and bottom of the garment. Then match and pin the rest of the curve, pinning at intervals of 4 in. to 5 in. (see the photo above). Because you have clipped the concave curve, you have the flexibility to shape it around the second piece without struggling. Sew at ⅝ in. (The staystitching won't show on the right side of the garment because it is closer to the seam allowances than to the stitching line.)

3. Press the seam flat, then, if the fabric is lightweight, press the seam to one side. It is okay to press the seam open, but clip the second seam where necessary so that each seam allowance will lie flat.

tip *I find it is easier to press princess seams to one side rather than pressing them open.*

tip *Staystitching, then clipping a curved seam to match the opposite curve is a good technique to have in your bag of tricks.*

Constructing shoulder seams

"Sew back to front at shoulder seams" appears in many pattern instructions. If you are new to sewing, however, this instruction is not straightforward.

SEWING SHOULDER SEAMS To sew the shoulder seams, take the back fabric piece and lay it on

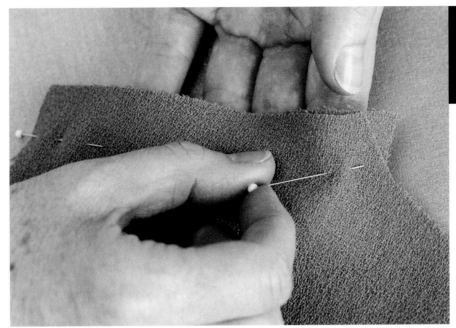

Note that the edges of "back to front at shoulder seams" don't match, but the seams do match ⅝ in. from the edge where you are going to sew them.

a flat surface right side up, then take the front fabric piece and lay it on top of the back piece with right sides together. Match the two top seams, which are the shoulder seams.

You will notice that the neck edges don't always match. The back neck edge at the shoulder is curved up and the front neck edge at the shoulder is curved in. In this instance, match the pieces at ⅝ in. from the edge (see the photo above). Pin and stitch, backstitching at the beginning and end of the seamline.

STABILIZING SHOULDER SEAMS You will also notice that the shoulder seams slant, which means that they are not on the straight grain and may stretch, especially if you are working with knits. If you are working with stretchy fabric, you should stabilize the shoulder seamline, using narrow, clear elastic.

To stabilize the seam, cut a piece of elastic the length of the shoulder seam, using the pattern piece as your guide. After pinning the seam along the ⅝-in. seamline, place the elastic on the line of pins. Repin, matching the ends of the elastic with each end of the seam and centering the elastic along the seamline. With the elastic side up, sew the seam and the elastic (see the left photo on p. 95). Press the seams open, and finish the seams if you wish. (See "Seam Finishes" on p. 94.)

tip *Don't press directly on top of clear elastic. Although most elastic can be pressed, the type used for stabilizing shoulder seams requires a much lower heat setting. You are safer using a press cloth or pressing from the other side.*

When sewing a garment, you have the option of leaving the seams unfinished or finishing them. You may simply want to zigzag or over-lock the edges, which will prevent raveling, one of the main reasons to finish a seam. Or you may want to challenge yourself to create a garment that looks good on the inside as well as on the outside. Here are two seam finishes that can be used on easy tops and dresses.

Flat-fell seams

A classic sewn finish that lends itself to easy tops and dresses is the flat-fell seam, especially on the shoulder seams. Even if the rest of the seams in the garment are left unfinished, flat-fell seams on these short seam allowances keep the seam allowances flat and hide the raw edges. Construct a flat-fell seam as follows:

1. After sewing and pressing open the seam allowance, trim ⅜ in. on one side of the seam allowance.

2. Press the untrimmed seam allowance over the trimmed seam allowance, then press in half, tuck-ing the trimmed seam allowance under the untrimmed one. Pin or pin and baste the folded seam allowance along the folded edge.

3. Turn the garment right side up. Flip the pins to the right side of the garment, then topstitch the folded seam allowance in place along the folded edge, following the basting line or the line of pins. The stitching line should be parallel to the seam.

Mock-fell seams

Another seam finish to consider is a mock-fell seam. This seam finish also controls raveling but

takes less time (and a little less skill) to construct than a classic flat-fell seam. Construct a mock-fell seam as follows:

1. After sewing and pressing open the seams, trim ¼ in. on one side of the seam allowance. Pink, over-lock, or zigzag the untrimmed seam allowance or leave it unfinished.

2. Press the untrimmed seam allowance over the trimmed one and pin.

3. Sew the untrimmed seam allowance down, keeping the stitching line parallel to the seam-line. The trimmed seam allowance will be hidden by the stitched-down seam allowance. (Because it is easy to keep your stitches parallel to the seamline, it is not necessary to sew from the right side of the garment.)

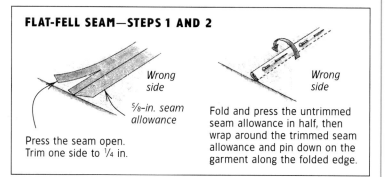

FLAT-FELL SEAM—STEPS 1 AND 2

Wrong side

⅝-in. seam allowance

Press the seam open. Trim one side to ¼ in.

Wrong side

Fold and press the untrimmed seam allowance in half, then wrap around the trimmed seam allowance and pin down on the garment along the folded edge.

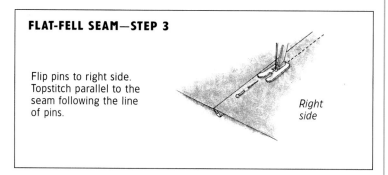

FLAT-FELL SEAM—STEP 3

Flip pins to right side. Topstitch parallel to the seam following the line of pins.

Right side

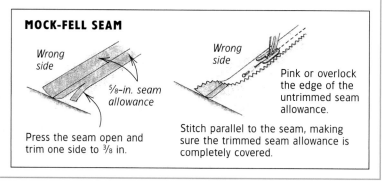

MOCK-FELL SEAM

Wrong side

⅝-in. seam allowance

Press the seam open and trim one side to ⅜ in.

Wrong side

Pink or overlock the edge of the untrimmed seam allowance.

Stitch parallel to the seam, making sure the trimmed seam allowance is completely covered.

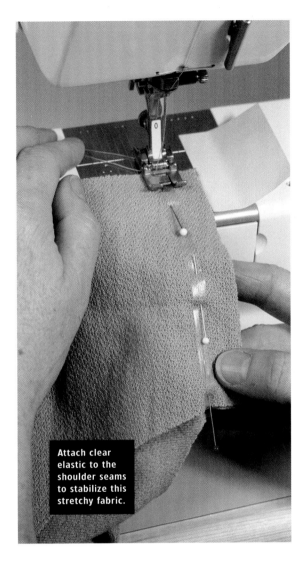

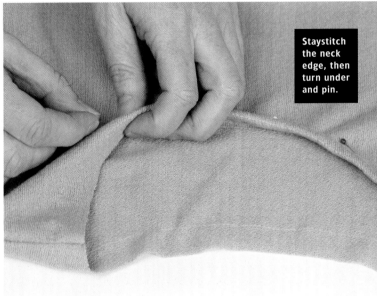

Attach clear elastic to the shoulder seams to stabilize this stretchy fabric.

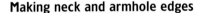

Making neck and armhole edges

Patterns for easy tops and dresses provide you with facing pieces for finishing the neck and armhole edges. However, you don't often find facings on ready-to-wear garments, and you don't find facings at all on knit garments. You find binding, lining, or, on knits especially, overlocked edges or ribbing but no facings. If you want the garments you are making to look like ready-to-wear, you have to ignore the fac-

ing pieces and follow a different path. I'll give you some options.

FOR KNITS ONLY, METHOD ONE If you are making a T-shirt in a knit fabric, one simple alternative to facing the neck and armhole edges is turning and topstitching using a single row of stitches or a double row of stitches made with a double needle.

1. Begin by staystitching the neck or armhole edge (see the right photo above). Staystitching is sewing through one layer of fabric a little less than ⅝ in. from the edge. Use a bit of staystitch-plus (see "Staystitch-Plus" on p. 68) to help shape the curved parts of these edges.

2. Press the neck or armhole edge to the wrong side of the garment, using the staystitching line as your guide. Pin it in place.

3. Working on the right side of the garment, topstitch the edge ⅜ in. from the fold (see the left photo on p. 96).

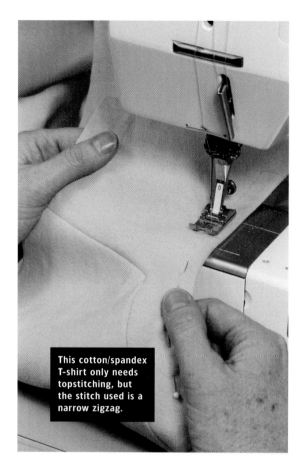

This cotton/spandex T-shirt only needs topstitching, but the stitch used is a narrow zigzag.

Using a double needle is a great finish, not only for the neck edge but also for sleeve and garment hems. Use a narrow (0.5) zigzag on a knit.

tip *If you are sewing a knit fabric and your sewing machine doesn't have many stretch stitch options, leave the machine in the straight stitch mode but move the zigzag dial to 0.5. The narrow zigzag will accommodate the stretchiness of the fabric.*

tip *If you are working with a power knit like spandex or a knit blend, you may have to change the type of sewing-machine needle from a universal-shaped point to an H-S or an SUK point to prevent skipped stitches.*

FOR KNITS ONLY, METHOD TWO A double needle is not two separately attached needles but two needles joined to a single attachment arm. A double needle uses two needle threads that are threaded side by side. Because there is only one bobbin thread, though, the stitches on the wrong side of the garment zigzag. If you are working with a knit, you can still set your machine to a narrow zigzag stitch to accommodate the stretch.

Follow the instructions in "For knits only, method one," but use a double needle to topstitch the curved neck or armhole edge. I like this finish so much that I use it for the garment and sleeve hems as well (see the right photo on the facing page).

FINISHING WITH A BIAS BAND, METHOD ONE This method, which works for both woven and knit fabric, is my favorite neck and armhole finish on an unlined, easy garment. For both types of fabric, I use strips of bias-cut fashion fabric. Bias has stretch that I use to shape the binding. Although knit fabric is already stretchy and has more stretch on the crosswise grain than on the lengthwise grain, I prefer using bias strips of knit fabric because it is actually less stretchy than crossgrain strips. (See "Make Your Own Bias Strips" on p. 98.)

1. Begin by cutting a piece of bias that is 1½ in. wide and as long as the neck or armhole edges. You may have to seam shorter pieces together.

2. Measure the curved edge you are going to bind. The bias strip will stretch, so the binding needs to be smaller than the neck or armhole edge. If the curved seam is 22 in., for instance, cut a piece that is 21 in. long and seam it in a circle using a ¼-in. seam allowance.

3. With right sides together, place the circle around the curved seam; match and pin the edges around the neck or armhole edge, using a ⅝-in. seam allowance. Sew.

The neckline on this knit top is finished with a bias band.

Bias is the direction between the straight grains—the lengthwise grain, which is parallel to the selvage, and the crosswise grain. The diagonal line directly between these two straight grains is the true bias; it is at a 45° angle from each straight grain (see the top illustration below).

Bias stretches and true bias stretches even more. This stretchiness is what makes bias strips the best choice for finishing neckline and armhole edges of garments.

Binding made with bias strips lays flat, looks great, and eliminates bulk.

Making bias strips is not difficult. Here are two methods you can use.

Preparing the fabric

For both methods, you will need to prepare the fabric first.

1. Lay a piece of fabric on a flat surface. The selvage edge is the first straight grain, the cut edge is the second.

2. If the cut edge is uneven, straighten it by placing a wide ruler along the selvage edge with the

bottom of the ruler across the cut edge. Draw a thin line along the bottom of the ruler, then turn the ruler and make the line longer. In this manner, the wide ruler is used like an artist's T-square.

If you're fussy, you can straighten the cut edge by pulling a thread across the fabric and cutting along the pulled thread (see the bottom illustration at left).

Method one

In this method, you will cut one strip at a time. I usually cut 2-in. strips because they are easier to work with than narrower ones. I would rather cut away excess fabric than fuss with small strips.

1. Once you have the piece of fabric squared up, mark and cut the strips of bias. To mark the bias, start at one corner of the fabric, for instance the lower left. If you need an 18-in. strip, mark a point 18 in. up from the corner along the selvage, and mark another 18 in. out from the corner along the cut edge. Using your ruler, draw a line between the two points, then mark a parallel second line 2 in. from the first (see the top left illustration on the facing page).

2. Cut along the lines. Violà! A bias strip.

Method two

A second method of finding bias allows you to cut two strips at once.

1. After squaring the fabric, take one corner and fold it toward the other straight edge of the fabric until it is parallel to that edge. The diagonal that is folded is the

FINDING THE BIAS

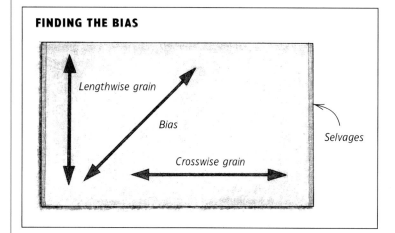

Lengthwise grain

Bias

Crosswise grain

Selvages

SQUARING UP THE FABRIC BY CUTTING ALONG A PULLED THREAD

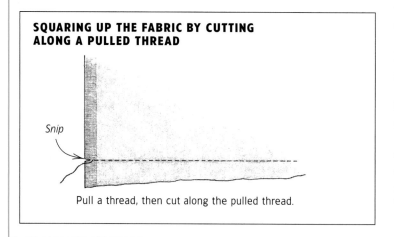

Snip

Pull a thread, then cut along the pulled thread.

bias (see the bottom illustration below).

2. Mark a line close to the fold and mark a parallel line 2 in. away.

3. Cut along the lines. Once again, perfect bias strips.

Seaming bias strips

Sometimes it is necessary to seam bias strips together to make a strip long enough to bind the edge of a garment. Seaming bias strips is not difficult. Ignore any pointed edges,

and place the bias strips right sides together. Because the strips stretch, pin the edges together before sewing straight across (see the top right illustration below).

FINDING THE BIAS—METHOD 1

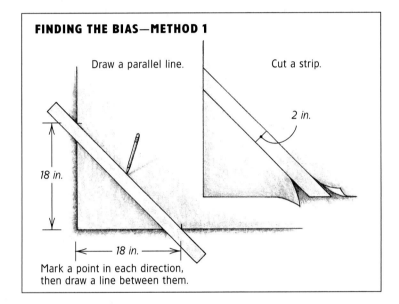

Draw a parallel line.

Cut a strip.

2 in.

18 in.

18 in.

Mark a point in each direction, then draw a line between them.

SEAMING BIAS STRIPS

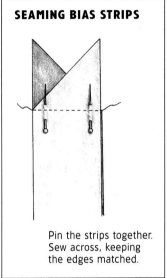

Pin the strips together. Sew across, keeping the edges matched.

FINDING THE BIAS—METHOD 2

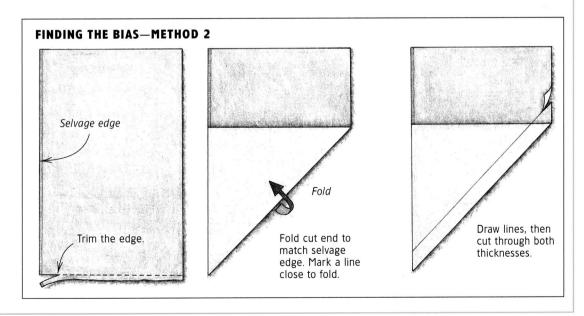

Selvage edge

Trim the edge.

Fold

Fold cut end to match selvage edge. Mark a line close to fold.

Draw lines, then cut through both thicknesses.

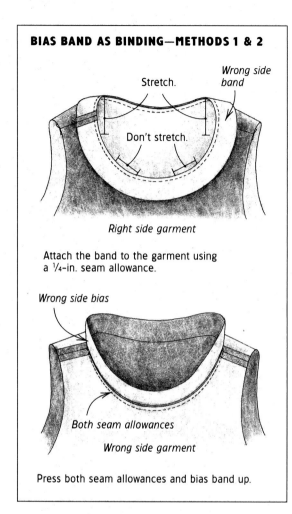

BIAS BAND AS BINDING—METHODS 1 & 2

Stretch.

Wrong side band

Don't stretch.

Right side garment

Attach the band to the garment using a ¼-in. seam allowance.

Wrong side bias

Both seam allowances

Wrong side garment

Press both seam allowances and bias band up.

4. Trim the seam allowances to ¼ in. and press the binding and the seam allowances to the wrong side. Pin.

5. Working on the right side of the garment, topstitch close to the curved edge to anchor the binding. If you don't want topstitching on your garment, anchor the binding to the shoulder seams and, on an armhole edge, to the side seams.

6. On the wrong side of the garment, trim excess binding. Because the facing is bias, it won't ravel, so it doesn't need an edge finish.

FINISHING WITH A BIAS BAND, METHOD TWO The second method for finishing with a bias band, which also works for knits and wovens, is to use it as a binding (see the photo on p. 97). Follow steps 1–3 of "Finishing with a bias band, method one."

4. Trim the seam allowance to ¼ in. and press the binding toward the seam allowances.

5. Press the band over the seam allowances to the wrong side, then pin (see the top left illustration on the facing page).

6. Working on the right side of the garment, stitch in the ditch to anchor the binding (see "Stitch in the Ditch" on p. 44).

7. On the wrong side of the garment, trim any excess binding below the stitching (see the top right illustration on the facing page).

FINISHING WITH A BIAS BAND, METHOD THREE The last method for finishing with a bias band is most like binding. Follow steps 1–3 of "Finishing with a bias band, method one" and step 4 of "Finishing with a bias band, method two."

> **tip** *When using a bias band as binding, I seam the band to the garment using a ¼-in. seam allowance rather than ⅝ in. Unless the garment has a high neck or tight sleeves, I find there is enough play in the pattern for me to deviate from the ⅝-in. seam allowance.*

BIAS BAND AS BINDING—METHOD 2

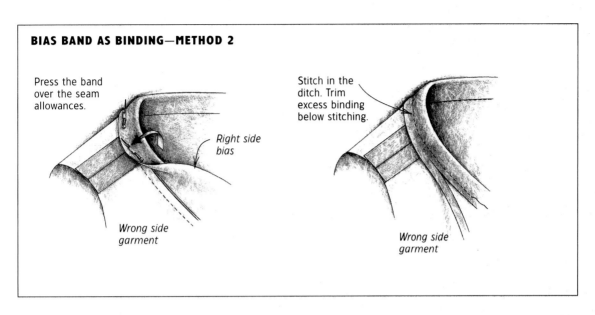

Press the band over the seam allowances.

Right side bias

Wrong side garment

Stitch in the ditch. Trim excess binding below stitching.

Wrong side garment

BIAS BAND AS BINDING—METHOD 3

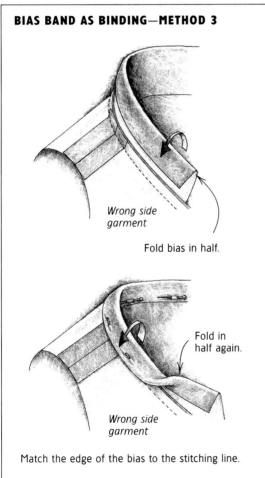

Wrong side garment

Fold bias in half.

Fold in half again.

Wrong side garment

Match the edge of the bias to the stitching line.

METHOD 3—FINISHING

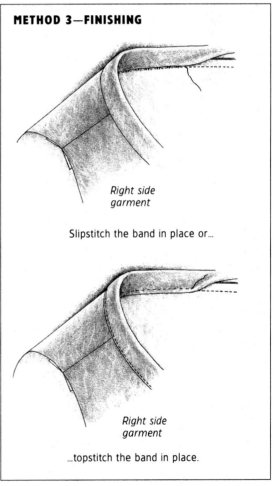

Right side garment

Slipstitch the band in place or...

Right side garment

...topstitch the band in place.

Facings are interfaced then sewn together to create one piece that is attached to the garment.

5. Looking at the wrong side of the band, fold the unsewn edge of the band in half toward the seam allowances and press. Unfold and press the unsewn half in half again (see the bottom left illustration on p. 101).

6. Fold the pressed underside of the binding over the attached side, matching the attachment seam with the folded edge.

7. Topstitch along the band or slipstitch by hand to keep it in place (see the bottom right illustration on p. 101). For more on slipstitching, see "Slipstitching" on p. 118.

FACINGS Facings are fabric pieces that are the same shape and size as the neck or armhole but only a couple of inches wide. You will find facings along the front of garment styles that button in the front and similarly in the back of garments that button in the back. Facings are also used to finish skirts or pants that have contour waistbands.

1. Begin by transferring all markings from the pattern to the fabric. Since the facing is the same shape and size as the edge of the pattern piece, it should be marked identically with notches, dots, and shapes. Most facings found in tops are small enough pieces so that there are no darts, pleats, or seams other than the shoulder seams (see the photo above).

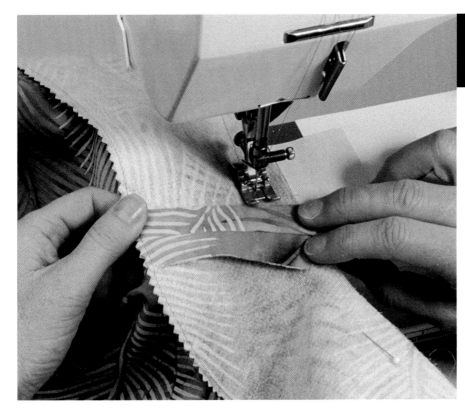

Attach the interfaced facing to the garment with right sides together after finishing the raw edge.

2. With right sides together, sew the front facing to the back facing along the shoulder seams and side seams. Before attaching the facing to the garment, finish the unnotched edge by using a zigzag or overlock stitch, by binding the edge, or by stitching and pinking.

3. Again with right sides together, place the facing along the matching garment edge. Pin and sew using a ⅝-in. seam allowance, then press the facing toward the seam allowances (see the photo above).

4. Understitch the facing (see the photo at right) by sewing both seam allowances to the facing ⅛ in. from the attachment seam (see the illustration on p. 106). Trim and grade the seams.

To understitch, press both seam allowances toward the facing and stitch through all layers of fabric about ⅛ in. from the attachment seam. Take care to keep the facing and the seam allowances flat under the needle.

Some patterns combine the neck and armhole facings. These are sewn to the garment, leaving the shoulder seams unsewn.

5. Press the facing to the wrong side of the garment. The understitching weights the seam and helps to keep it flat. This technique is much like the one described in the second method of finishing the bias band on p. 100.

For neck and armhole edges on easy T-shirts and pullover tops, I prefer finishing with a bias band. But for other tops and dresses with front openings, facings are a must.

COMBINATION NECK AND ARMHOLE FACINGS Patterns for sleeveless dresses often feature a one-piece facing to finish the neck and armhole edge. This facing is constructed as follows.

1. With right sides together, sew the front facing to the back facing at the side seams. Do not sew the shoulder seams. The shoulder seams on the garment are also left unsewn.

2. Match and pin the facing to the neck and armhole edges of the garment, stopping ¾ in. from each shoulder seam (see the photo above).

3. Sew the pinned edges using a ⅝-in. seam allowance.

4. Understitch the facing as much as possible, keeping the area under the sewing machine as flat as possible. You won't be able to get all the way up to the shoulders.

5. Trim, grading the seam allowances. Press the faced neck and armhole edges.

6. With right sides together and keeping the facing shoulder seam allowances out of the way, sew the garment shoulder seams at ⅝ in. Tuck in one facing shoulder seam and turn under the second. Topstitch from the right side of the garment along the shoulder seam (a type of stitching in the ditch), or hand-slipstitch the

The neckline of this V-neck t-shirt is finished with a facing.

FINISHING A V-NECK WITH A BAND—STEP 1

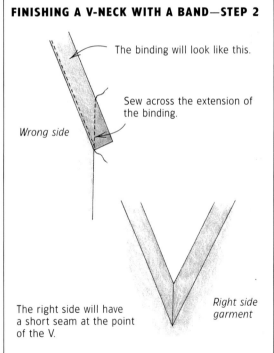

Before sewing, staystitch ½ in. on each side of the point of the V. Clip to but not through V.

FINISHING A V-NECK WITH A BAND—STEP 2

The binding will look like this.

Sew across the extension of the binding.

Wrong side

The right side will have a short seam at the point of the V.

Right side garment

facing shoulder seams on the wrong side of the garment (see "Slipstitching" on p. 118).

V-NECK WITH A BAND V-necks may be finished with either a band or a facing. Here is how to finish one with a band.

1. Before applying a band, staystitch the V part of the V-neck. Because you are going to clip into the seam allowance at the V, staystitch with smaller than usual stitches ½ in. on each side of the V. To staystitch, sew through one layer of fabric, keeping the sewing-machine needle down in the point of the V, lifting the presser foot and turning the garment, then lowering the presser foot and sewing about ½ in. far-

ther. Clip to but not through the V (see the top illustration above), then follow the instructions given in "Finishing with a bias band, method one" on p. 99. Clipping the V allows you to bind the area of the V as if it were a straight line.

2. After binding the neck edge, turn the garment inside out and fold the neckline in half with right sides together. Above the V you will see that the band extends beyond the center front of the garment. Sew a straight line across this bit of band. The line should extend up from the center front of the garment to the edge of the band (see the bottom illustration on p. 105).

V-NECK WITH A FACING Instead of finishing a V-neck with a band, here is how you can finish it with a facing.

1. With right sides together, sew the front neck facing to the back neck facing at the shoulder seams. Press the seams open.

2. Again with right sides together, match and pin the facing to the neck edge. Sew using a ⅝-in. seam allowance, but shorten the stitch length for ½ in. on each side of the V. Clip to but not through the V.

3. Press the facing toward the seam allowances. Understitch the facing by sewing the facing to the seam allowances, ⅛ in. from the attachment seam (see the illustration at right). You will not be able to sew continuously from one end of the facing to the other because of the V; you will have to work one side of the neck edge, then the other.

4. Trim and grade the seams, then press the facing to the wrong side of the garment. The understitching weights the seam and helps to keep it flat.

Easy sleeves

Putting a sleeve in a simple garment is not a difficult task, and learning expands the opportunity for making more garment styles.

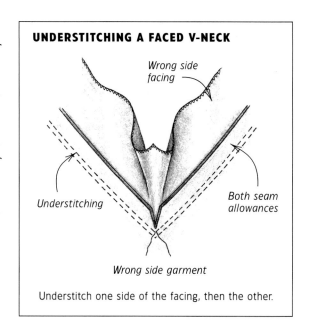

UNDERSTITCHING A FACED V-NECK

Wrong side facing

Understitching

Both seam allowances

Wrong side garment

Understitch one side of the facing, then the other.

SHIRT SLEEVES Easy tops have the easiest sleeves. When a sleeve is added to a garment, it is called setting a sleeve. Easy sleeves are set in the garment after the garment front and garment back are joined at the shoulder seams but before the side seams are sewn. By easing the sleeve, you will be able to match the sleeve's curved edge to the garment armhole edge, the area called the armscye.

The sleeve pattern piece is distinctive. It has a curve in the center called the sleeve cap, the highest point of which lines up with the shoulder seam. Look for the dot or line that marks the center of the sleeve cap. There are also two concave curves, one on each side of the sleeve cap. These match the armhole at the front and back of the garment. The curves are not the same; the back is generally longer and slightly less concave than the front. Look for two notches on the back of the sleeve and one notch on the front of the sleeve. There also

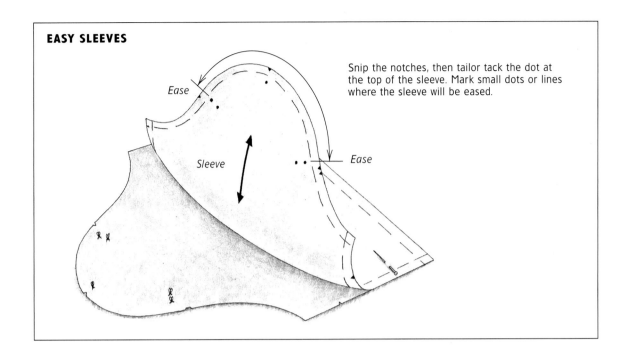

EASY SLEEVES

Ease

Sleeve

Ease

Snip the notches, then tailor tack the dot at the top of the sleeve. Mark small dots or lines where the sleeve will be eased.

may be small dots on the pattern piece or double rows of lines.

1. Before setting in a sleeve, transfer all markings from the pattern to the fabric, including notches, dots, ease points, and the top of the sleeve. For notches and lines, snip the seam allowances ⅛ in., and for dots and shapes, use tailor tacks, chalk, or other markers (see the illustration above).

2. The sleeve pattern will tell you to "ease between notches" or "ease" and instruct you to make parallel rows of long stitches that you will pull to ease the fabric. This is the old-fashioned way to ease a sleeve cap. The modern method of easing is to place a single layer of fabric under the needle of the sewing machine. Working about ½ in. from the edge, put your finger behind the presser foot and press against the fabric as you sew. Your finger will act as a dam, preventing the fabric from moving freely

through the machine, thus crimping, or easing, the cap of the sleeve (see "Staystitch-Plus" on p. 68). In general, sleeves in easy tops don't need too much ease (see the top photo on p. 108).

3. Lay the garment right side up on a flat surface. Begin matching the sleeve to the garment right sides together by matching the dot that marks the top of the sleeve cap to the shoulder seam. Working out toward each side seam, match and pin the pieces. The pieces will not lie flat but the edges should match (see the bottom photo on p. 108). If you find the pieces don't match, there are two solutions. If the sleeve is too big, go back and staystitch-plus some more. If the sleeve is too small, pop some of the stitches or press out some of the staystitch-plus. When the edges match, stitch using a ⅝-in. seam allowance.

4. If the fabric is stretchy, you may want to add piece of clear elastic or Seams Great to

Ease the cap of a sleeve using staystitch-plus.

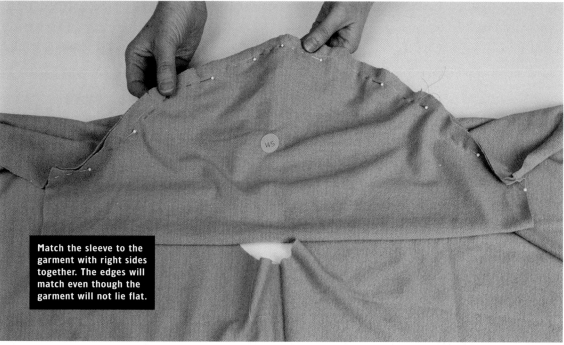

Match the sleeve to the garment with right sides together. The edges will match even though the garment will not lie flat.

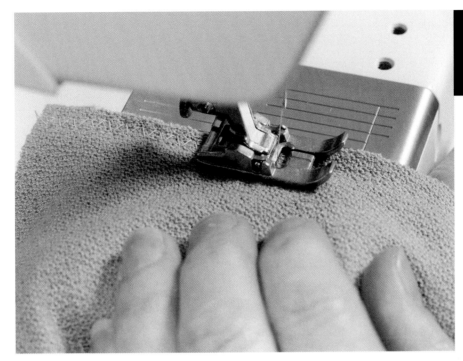

stabilize the seamline. You can attach the stabilizer as you set the sleeve by adding the elastic to the matched and pinned sleeve edge. Pin the elastic down the center of the seamline, then sew at ⅝ in. through all layers.

5. Sew a second row of stitches next to the first, and press the seam allowances toward the garment. For knit fabrics, trim the seam allowance to ¼ in. Zigzag the seam allowance edges together, and press them toward the garment (see the photo above).

6. Finish the sleeve sides and the garment side seams at the same time. Turn the garment so that right sides are together, then match and pin the underarm seam of the sleeve and the side seam of the garment. Sew using a ⅝-in. seam allowance.

RAGLAN SLEEVES A raglan sleeve is a two-piece sleeve that has a seam down the center of the arm. Each sleeve piece is curved to match the armscye along the garment front and garment back. The curved seams and the center seam meet at the neck edge of the garment (see the illustration on p. 110). Here is how to construct this easy sleeve.

1. Match and pin the sleeve front to the sleeve back along the long center seam. Sew using a ⅝-in. seam allowance.

2. Next, match and pin the sleeve front to the garment along the armscye, then sew using a ⅝-in. seam allowance. Finally, match and pin the sleeve back to the garment back along the armscye. Again, sew using a ⅝-in. seam allowance.

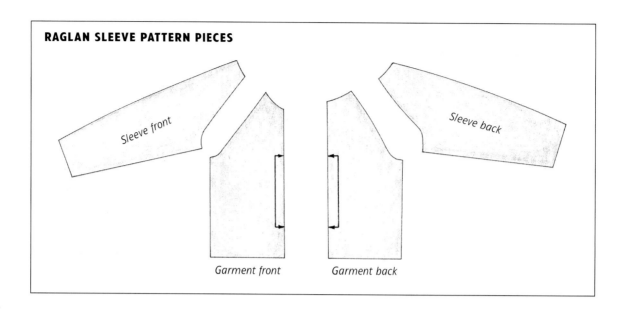

RAGLAN SLEEVE PATTERN PIECES

Sleeve front

Sleeve back

Garment front

Garment back

This simple T-shirt is finished at the neck edge, the sleeve hems, and the bottom hem by machine using a double needle.

Hemming

If you have constructed an easy garment on the sewing machine, there is no reason to hem the garment by hand unless you have a real aversion to topstitching. Hemming by machine appears on all sorts of garments made of all sorts of fabrics, from sheers to wools.

1. Trim the uneven edges before folding up the hem, then try on the garment to determine the length you like.

2. Fold excess fabric to the wrong side of the garment and pin in place.

3. Take the garment off, lay it on a flat surface, and line up the front and back along the shoulder seams.

4. Measure the hem you have marked, then pin the hem evenly around the garment using a small seam guide. Machine-stitched hems vary in depth—½ in. to 2 in. are common. Mark the depth of the hem with pins or chalk, plus ¼ in. if you need to finish the edge. Trim excess fabric.

5. Try the garment on again after you have pinned the hem to make sure it's right.

6. Sew the hem in place from the right side of the garment. If you have folded back a 1-in. hem, sew at ¾ in.; if you have folded back ⅝ in., sew at ½ in. This ensures that you have attached the hem. To help you sew straight, use a Post-It note or another marking device on the sewing machine.

If you want to hand-stitch a hem, follow steps 1-5 of the machine-stitching instructions, above. Then, choose a needle that is the smallest that will pass through your fabric, since too big a needle would leave holes. Thread a needle with a single thread and knot it. Don't put too much thread on the needle or it's sure to tangle. Sitting in a well-lit place and working on the wrong side of the garment, hem the garment using a fell stitch (see p. 74), a blindstitch (see p. 74), or a blind catchstitch (see p. 75).

tip *The hem edges of lightweight woven fabrics can be folded twice before topstitching. Press ¼ in. or ½ in. to the wrong side of the fabric, then fold and press the hem. If folding under this much makes the hem edge bulky, however, finish the edge by serging it or binding it with rayon seam tape. You could also construct a Hong Kong finish (see p. 38).*

■ EASY VESTS

Sewing an easy vest uses many of the sewing techniques discussed in the first part of this chapter: marking the fabric, sewing darts or princess seams, and sewing shoulder seams. Constructing an easy vest follows that construction sequence, adding a few new details for an easy garment with a bit of pizzazz.

There are a couple of flip-and-turn methods for sewing a vest. I think this one is the easiest. (See "Constructing an Easy Vest" below.)

Cutting the pattern

To make this easy vest, you will need to cut fabric for the vest front pattern pieces and the vest back pattern pieces, the mock welt (if there is one), and the ties, or martingales. You won't need the facing pieces, so put those back into the pattern envelope. You also need to buy the same amount of fabric for the lining as you did for the vest.

> ### CONSTRUCTING AN EASY VEST
>
> • Cut out the fabric pieces.
> • Mark the fabric.
> • Prepare the ties.
> • Sew darts or princess seams.
> • Construct the mock welt.
> • Sew the shoulder seams.
> • Construct the lining.
> • Trim the lining.
> • Attach the lining to the fabric.
> • Sew the side seams.
> • Finish the vest.

To construct the mock welt, fold one seam allowance to the wrong side of the garment and press, then sew across each short end.

Constructing a mock welt

Mock welts are small, fake pockets that are often found on vests. They add detail to otherwise plain garments and are easy to construct.

1. Transfer the markings that indicate the end points of the mock welt from the pattern to the fabric by using either tailor tacks, chalk, or other markers.

2. Construct both mock welts at the same time. Press the ⅝-in. seam allowance on one of the long edges of the welt piece to the wrong side. Trim this folded-under edge to ⅜ in.

3. Fold the welt along the foldline with right sides together, then pin and sew along the remaining short edges using a ⅝-in. seam allowance (see the photo above). Trim the seam allowances to ¼ in., cutting a bit more off in the corners. Turn the welt right side out and press. Using a point turner, push the corners into shape, then press and pound the welt flat with a clapper if the welt is puffy.

4. Working on the right side of the garment with the right sides together, position the welt upside down, matching the ends of the welt with the end points you have marked on the garment (see the top photo on the facing page).

5. Pin and sew the welt's ⅝-in. seam allowance in place from end point to end point. Then sew a second row of stitches parallel to the first, about ¼ in. away (see the bottom photo on the facing page).

6. Carefully trim the seam allowance close to the second row of stitches. Slipstitch the foldline of the pressed-back seam allowance close to the attachment stitching.

7. Press the mock welt up over the stitching line toward the top of the garment. To attach the mock pocket along the short edges, either

Place the mock welt on the garment front with the finished edge toward the bottom of the garment.

On the mock welt, sew a second row of stitches.

> **tip** *If you machine-stitch through multiple thicknesses of fabric, it may be necessary to switch to a larger size needle so that the needle doesn't break.*

machine-stitch or hand-stitch the edges in place (see the top photo on p. 114).

8. Press the finished mock welt.

Constructing ties

Ties, which are called martingales in some vest patterns, are short belt pieces that cinch in the back of the vest. There are two types: ones that are attached in the side seam of the garment and tie in the center back (see the bottom photo on p. 114), and ones that are anchored in fitting details such as darts or princess seams and are cinched in with a small buckle. In either case, the first step is to sew the ties.

Machine-stitch the mock welt in place. Because there are several layers of fabric in the welt and the garment, switch to a bigger needle to prevent the needle from breaking.

The martingales add shape to a vest.

1. With right sides together, fold the fabric in half lengthwise. Sew across one short edge and the long edge, then trim close to the stitches, especially at the corner (see the photo on the facing page).

2. Using a pencil, a small ruler, the blunt end of a knitting needle, or your finger, turn this narrow band right side out. Press.

3. If the ties are anchored in fitting details such as darts or princess seams, sew them in place early in the construction sequence. When the garment is folded right sides together to construct the dart, place the tie into the folded-out fabric on the right side of the garment. Sewing the dart anchors the tie. Similarly, in a princess seam, pin the tie between the right sides of the garment pieces and anchor it in place with the seam.

If the ties are anchored in the side seams, add them later in the construction process when the vest side seams are sewn. Sew the ties in place between the fashion fabric vest front and vest back (if you pin them between the lining vest front and back they will end up on the inside of the vest).

Using a lining to finish a vest

The fastest and easiest vest to construct is the fully lined one that I describe here. The added bonus to adding a lining is that the garment looks as good on the inside as it does on the outside. Easy dresses can be constructed this way, too, but let's start with the vest.

1. After you have sewn the fashion fabric vest fronts to the fashion fabric vest back along the shoulder seams, set this half of the garment aside. Next, cut out and construct the pattern in lining fabric, just as you have the fashion fabric. Eliminate the mock welt, and sew the front to the back at the shoulder seams.

2. Once you have finished the lining, or inside vest, trim ⅛ in. from both armhole edges and from the front edges, starting near the side seam, going from the bottom front around the neck to the other side, and stopping near the side seam (see the top photo on p. 116).

> **tip** *If you are having trouble figuring out where the ties go, pin them in place, flip the garment to the right side, and check to see if you have it right.*

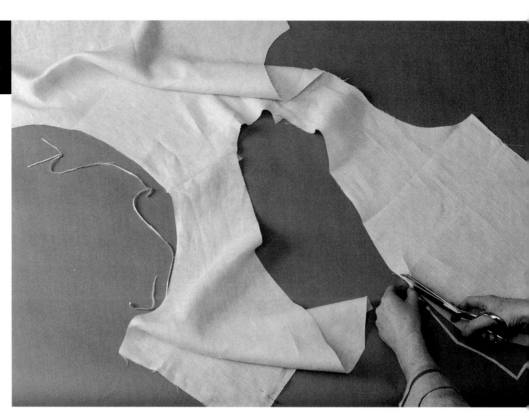

In this easy flip-and-turn vest construction, the armhole, front, and neck edges of the lining are trimmed ⅛ in.

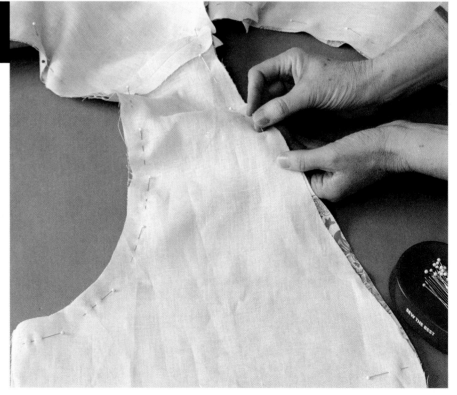

Match, pin, and sew the armhole, front, and neck edges, even though you have trimmed the lining.

Trim the seams you have sewn, then reach between the two layers from the back to turn the vest right side out.

3. Place the fashion fabric vest, or outside vest, right side up on a flat surface. Position the inside vest right side down on the outside vest, then pin the edges that you have trimmed, even if it seems hard (see the bottom photo on the facing page). It's okay if one piece curls, just as long as the edges are matched and pinned.

4. Sew, using a ⅝-in. seam allowance, then press and trim the seam allowances to ¼ in.

5. Next, reach between the vest backs and pull each side of the vest to the right side (see the photo above). Press, which is essential here.

6. Pin the fashion fabric to the fashion fabric along the side seam, placing the martingale between these two pieces, then pin the lining to the lining along the side seam. Sew where you have pinned, all along the fashion fabric side seam and along the lining fabric side seam

(see the photo on p. 118). The seam will be U-shaped.

7. Press the seams open.

8. Press the bottom, unsewn edges of the outside vest up ⅝ in., then press the bottom, unsewn edges of the inside vest up a bit more so that it won't show from the right side of the

tip *If your sewing machine has a free arm, now is the time to use it. As you sew the vest side seams, it is important to keep the part of the vest that is under the needle flat so that other parts don't get caught in the stitches. Use your fingers to keep the top flat, and check the underside of the work with your thumbs.*

To sew the side seams, match fashion fabric to fashion fabric and lining to lining. The ties go between the fashion fabric pieces.

SLIPSTITCHING

Slipstitching, which can be used to finish edges, is done by hand. To do this, thread a needle with double thread and knot the end. Turn the garment so that the work is below where you are stitching. In our example of sewing a vest with a lining, work on the inside, or lining side.

The stitches go from right to left. Push the needle through the folded edge of the lining to bury the knot, then take a tiny stitch in the fashion fabric and pull the needle out (see the illustration at right). When you take tiny stitches in the fashion fabric, try to get just a thread or two so that the stitches won't be visible on the right side of the garment. Come across to the lining side, and take another tiny stitch. Repeat two or three stitches. Slightly pull the thread, which will cause the pieces to turn in toward each other. Repeat across the open area, then knot the thread at the end of the line of stitches and bury the knot.

SLIPSTITCH

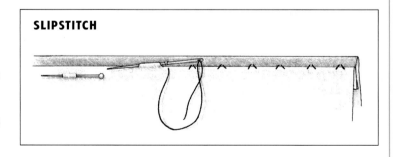

fabric. Topstitch or slipstitch the edges together. (See "Slipstitching" on the facing page.)

■ FINISHING OTHER GARMENTS WITH A LINING

When sewing sleeveless dresses and tops, finishing with a lining rather than with facings or bindings is both fast and good looking. To do this, construct the fashion fabric garment: Make darts or princess seams, attach the front to the back at the shoulder seams, but don't sew the side seams and don't insert the zipper. Construct the lining following the same steps.

1. With right sides together, place the fashion fabric garment on the lining garment. Match and pin the neck and armhole edges, then sew at ⅝ in.

2. Understitch the neck and armhole edges, as if the lining were a facing (see the illustration on p. 106). It might not be possible to understitch all the way around the armhole edges or around the neck edge, but sew as far as you can. Use your fingers to help you keep the work flat under the needle (see the photo above). Trim the seam allowances carefully, grading the seams.

3. After the lining is attached, sew the side seams, then pull the lining out of the way of the fashion fabric seam allowance and insert the zipper. Once the zipper is in, press under the ⅝-in. seam allowance on the lining, position it along each side of the zipper tape. Pin, then slipstitch in place by hand.

easy shirts
and blouses

■ ■ 4 ■

When I started to sew, I never made shirts and blouses because I didn't know how to make buttonholes. Then I began to make the kind of shirts that could be fastened with a big pin at the neck and a small safety pin to hold the front together (I would roll up the sleeves). Now that I have conquered my fear of buttonholes, I love shirts and blouses and want you to, too.

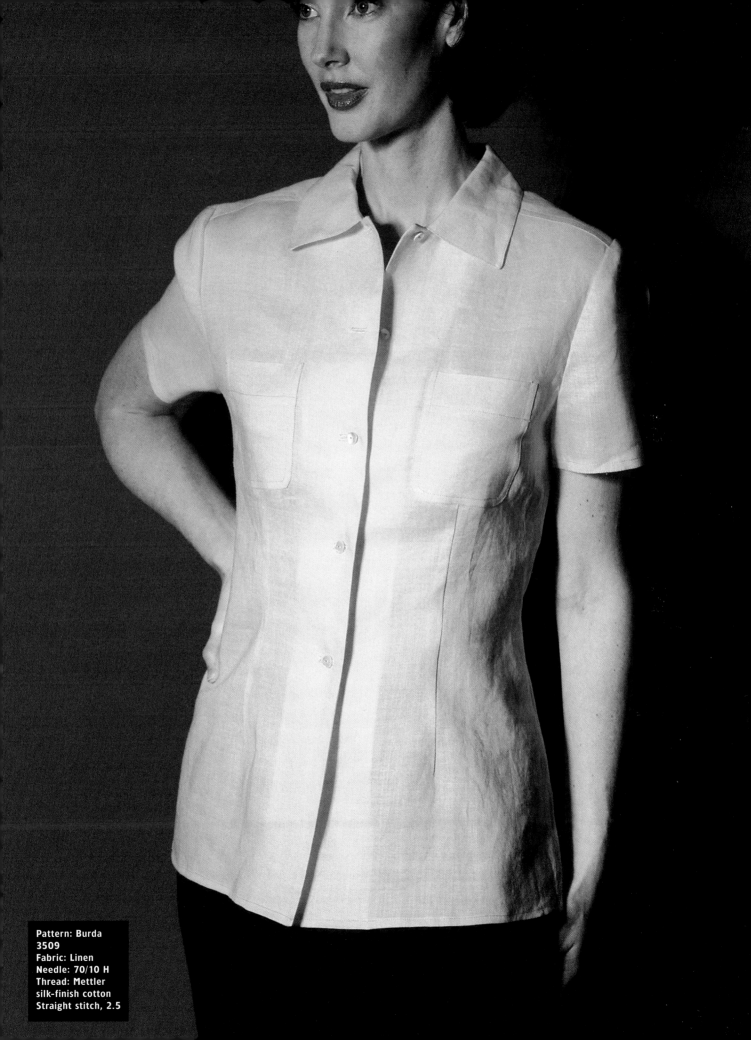

Pattern: Burda
3509
Fabric: Linen
Needle: 70/10 H
Thread: Mettler
silk-finish cotton
Straight stitch, 2.5

Stage I: Project preparation
- Buy the fabric, interfacing, and pattern.
- Check and alter fit as needed.
- Prepare the fabric.
- Cut and mark the pieces.
- Interface the collar and facings.

Stage II: Shaping the pieces
- Sew darts or princess seams.
- Add patch pockets.
- Sew the front to the back at the shoulder seams.
- Prepare and attach the collar.

Stage III: Putting it all together
- Attach the facings.
- Hem the pieces.
- Sew the side seams.
- Set in the sleeves.

Stage IV: Finishing
- Make buttonholes.
- Sew on buttons.

To me, it's the fabric that distinguishes a great blouse or shirt. I always think of Hawaiian shirts from the 1930s and '40s and find myself looking at the rayon prints that are reminiscent of those great classic shirts. You're sure to see other prints that evoke the phrase, "Wouldn't that make a great shirt?" There are silks, fine cottons and cotton lawns, oxford cloths, and shirtings that would make a closetful of great blouses, but stick to the more stable and less slippery ones until you have more practice.

Because shirts and blouses have many pieces (see the illustration on the facing page), some sewers are reluctant to start (or, let's face it, finish) such a project. But if you break the project up into small sections, the whole garment won't seem daunting. Follow the pattern instructions, but use the information here to help you interpret between the lines.

■ STAGE I: PROJECT PREPARATION

Getting ready to sew involves not only choosing the pattern and fabric but also washing the fabric, pressing it, cutting out the pattern pieces, and cutting out the fabric pieces. There

are always, of course, a few more things to do, such as interfacing the facings and collar.

Cutting and marking the fabric

After you have prepared your fabric and cut out the pattern pieces, cut the garment pieces. You will also need to cut interfacing for specific pieces. The ones that need interfacing are the facings, collar, and cuffs (if you are making a long sleeve blouse). There is rarely a separate pattern piece for the interfacing, so look for the instructions on the pattern itself. The pattern will tell you to "Cut 2 of fabric" and "Cut 2 of interfacing." The pattern instructions have a separate layout diagram for the pieces that need to be cut from interfacing.

After you have cut the fabric and interfacing, transfer the markings from the pattern to the fabric, including notches, which are the small triangles on the edges of the pattern pieces, and dots, which are matchpoints typically inside the edges of the pattern. If the pattern includes a pocket, look for the pocket placement mark. Indicated by a short line or an X, this mark needs to be transferred to the fabric,

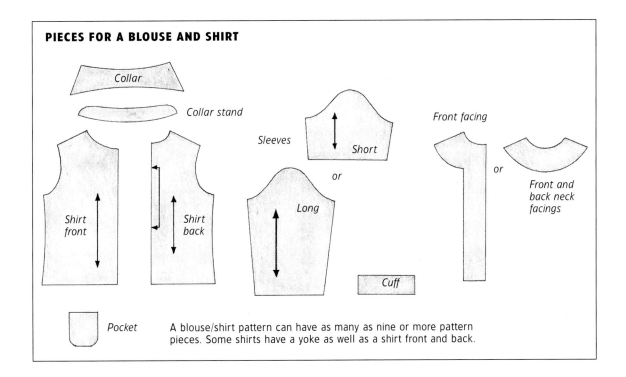

PIECES FOR A BLOUSE AND SHIRT

Collar

Collar stand

Sleeves

Short

or

Long

Cuff

Front facing

or

Front and back neck facings

Shirt front

Shirt back

Pocket

A blouse/shirt pattern can have as many as nine or more pattern pieces. Some shirts have a yoke as well as a shirt front and back.

too. I recommend that you transfer notches using small ⅛-in. snips, and dots and other important marks using tailor tacks, chalk, or marking pens.

If you're not sure you'll be able to distinguish the right side of the fabric from the wrong side, mark the wrong side by using peel-and-stick labels or by making a chalk mark.

Interfacing the collars and facings

If you have previously avoided using interfacing, you can't avoid it any longer. Collars need interfacing, as do the facings on shirts and blouses, since there will be buttons and buttonholes on the garment front.

For shirts and blouses, use lightweight interfacing: SofKnit and Touch-o-Gold are two that I look for, as well as fusible cotton batiste,

which is hard to find. Pellon Sof-Shape is an old standby for me. All of these are fusibles, although Touch-o-Gold fuses in place only lightly, making it a sort of temporary fusible. Nonfusibles to consider using are cotton batiste and silk organza (see also "Choosing Interfacing" on p. 124).

To interface the collar pieces, whether or not you're using a fusible, cut the interfacing pieces the same size as the collar. Place the interfacing on the wrong side of the collar pieces.

FUSING INTERFACING If you are using fusible interfacing, place the collar pieces on the ironing board with the wrong side up, and then place the interfacing glue side down on the collar pieces. Cover with a press cloth and spritz with water. Press, holding the iron in place for 10 seconds over the entire surface of

Interfacings for easy shirts and blouses include nonfusible cotton batiste (left) and fusible Sof-shape (top right) and Fusi-knit (bottom right).

CHOOSING INTERFACING

Learning to choose an interfacing is a task made easier by doing it over and over. Get in the habit of putting the fabric and interfacing together in your hand so that you can learn by feel. It's usually obvious what doesn't work—the stiff stuff, the cardboardy one, maybe even the crisp one if your fabric is more fluid. Ask the salesclerk at the fabric store which interfacing she uses. If she doesn't know, ask a friend who sews. The interfacings I've listed in the text are on my own shortlist of interfacings to use for shirts and blouses.

the piece. The pieces are small, so it doesn't take too much time.

SEWING IN INTERFACING If the interfacing is non-fusible, hand-baste each interfacing piece to each collar piece with even running stitches all around the edge. Stitch ⅜ in. to ¾ in. from the edge so the basting can be easily removed after the collar is constructed (see the bottom photo on the facing page).

CLEAN-FINISHING THE BACK NECK AND FRONT FACINGS
The best way to attach interfacing to the back neck and front facing is to clean-finish, or bag, the interfacing. Another description of this is "facing the facing." Whatever you wish to call it, you will like the way it looks on the inside of any blouse or shirt.

1. With right sides together, place the fabric front facing against the interfacing front facing.

Interfacing is cut the same size as the pattern piece. Place a press cloth on the ironing board, then the garment piece wrong side up, the interfacing resin side down, and a press cloth to cover. Spritz with water and press, holding down the iron 10 seconds each time.

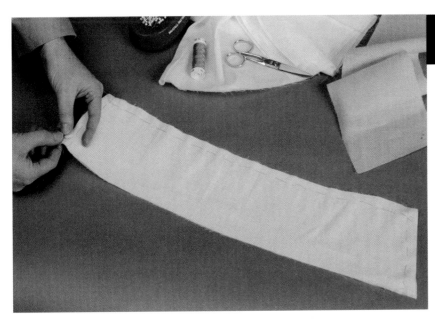

Hand-baste nonfusible interfacing all around the fashion fabric piece.

Pin the unnotched edge, which is *not* the edge that attaches to the front of the garment and the neck. Sew, using a narrow, ¼-in. seam (see the top illustration on p. 126).

2. Finger-press the seam allowance open, and then finger-press the seam allowance toward the interfacing. Fold the interfacing to the wrong side of the garment piece, and then match and pin all edges.

3. If you are using a fusible interfacing, press with an iron along the folded seam allowance so that wrong sides are together. Then place a press cloth over the piece, spritz with water, and fuse the entire piece (see the illustration

CLEAN-FINISHING A FACING—STEP 1

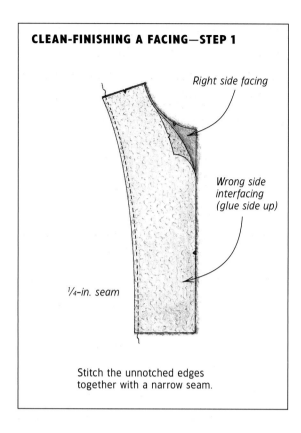

Right side facing

Wrong side interfacing (glue side up)

¼-in. seam

Stitch the unnotched edges together with a narrow seam.

tip *Finger pressing means that rather than pressing the seam open with the iron, you use your fingers. Just open the seam by hand and press with your fingers right along the seamline. This technique is especially successful with cottons.*

below). If you are using a sew-in interfacing, press the interfacing along the folded seam allowance so that wrong sides are together. Pin, then hand-baste ½ in. from all edges.

If there is a back neck facing piece, seam the fabric back neck facing to the fabric front facings at the shoulder seams before interfacing (see the illustration on the facing page). Seam

CLEAN-FINISHING A FACING—STEP 2

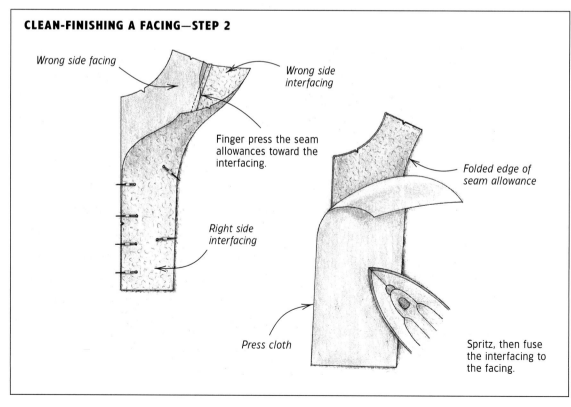

Wrong side facing

Wrong side interfacing

Finger press the seam allowances toward the interfacing.

Right side interfacing

Folded edge of seam allowance

Press cloth

Spritz, then fuse the interfacing to the facing.

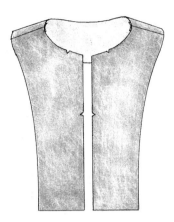

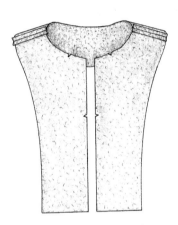

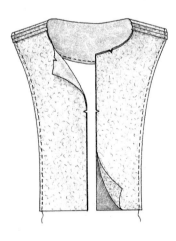

Sew the back neck facing to the front facings and the interfacing pieces together at the shoulder seams. Match, pin, and then sew the facing to the interfacing at the unnotched edges.

the interfacing pieces together as well, and then clean finish the entire joined piece as described previously. Trim the curved seam of the back neck facing close to the stitching line before turning it wrong sides together.

■ STAGE II: SHAPING THE PIECES

Think of a blouse or shirt as a collection of little puzzles that are eventually assembled into one piece. First, you have to make all the little puzzles—the fronts, back, collar, and cuffs. Once the pieces are interfaced, it's time to start assembling them.

Sewing darts

Darts are fitting elements that give shape to a garment. Found in skirts, slacks, dresses, shirts, and blouses, darts appear on pattern pieces as triangles. When sewn, darts pinch out more fabric at one end than at the other. These fitting elements point to fuller parts of the body: in shirts and blouses, they point to the bust. Darts are sewn first in the construction process.

1. Transfer the triangular shape of a dart from the pattern to the wrong side of the fabric using a tracing wheel and tracing paper, tailor tacks, chalk, or a combination of snips and tailor tacks or chalk (see the illustrations on p. 89).

I use the combination method. I make small snips at the edge of the garment to indicate the outer edge of the dart, and I make tailor tacks at the dart point. If the dart is long, I mark the midpoint of each side.

Complete the foldover collar by sewing across the short ends.

3. If your pattern does not have a back neck facing, the pattern instructions will tell you to press under the center of the ⅝-in. seam allowance of the upper collar. Trim the pressed-back seam allowance.

4. Machine-baste the collar in place along the neck edge of the shirt, matching notches and dots. Take care not to catch any of the pressed-under edge. The collar will be permanently anchored in place when the facings are attached.

ONE-PIECE COLLARS A one-piece collar actually has two pieces: the upper collar and the under collar. This collar is distinguished from the more difficult-to-construct two-piece collar, which is a collar with a collar stand.

1. Interface one or both collar pieces. If you have interfaced only one, this piece should be designated the upper collar. Otherwise, choose one to be the under collar and trim ⅛ in. off the unnotched edges. The unnotched edges are the two short sides and the one long side that doesn't attach to the neck edge (see the top photo on the facing page).

2. Pin and match the under collar to the upper collar, right sides together. Even though the under collar is smaller since you trimmed it, match the edges.

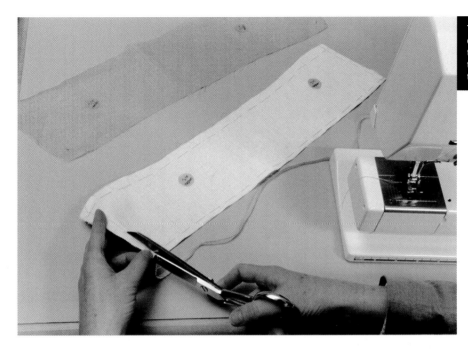

> **tip** *Fold each collar piece in half and make a small snip in the center on the notched and unnotched edges of each piece. You can use these as additional matchpoints when you assemble the collar and when you attach it to the shirt.*

3. Sew the pinned edges. To make the collar points, pivot and sew across each collar point two or three stitches, then pivot again at the adjoining seamline (see the photo at right). Do this at both collar points. (This makes room for the seam allowances on the inside. If you sew just to the point and pivot, the seam allowances are crammed into too small a space and the collar points look more like wads than points. This is a good technique to have in your bag of tricks.)

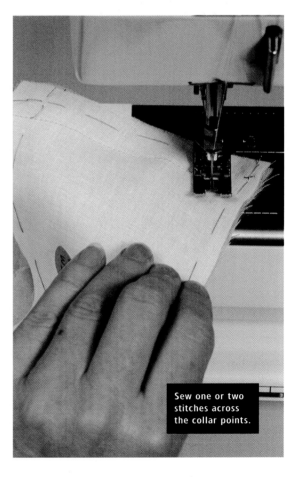

Sew one or two stitches across the collar points.

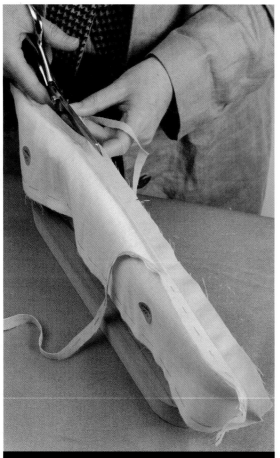

Press the collar seam open, and then grade the seam allowances so that the seam allowance closest to the upper collar is wider than the one closest to the under collar.

tip *I admit that I grade seams a little closer than ¼ in. and ⅜ in.; I grade them more like ⅛ in. and ¼ in. As a beginner, I recommend starting wider until you are a more confident trimmer.*

4. Press, then trim the seam allowances and grade them if the fabric is thick. Grading the seam allowances is cutting them so that they are graduated in width. The seam allowance that is closest to the top of the collar is wider, so trim it to ⅜ in. The seam allowance closest to the under collar is narrower, so trim it to ¼ in. (see the photo at left). Trim close to the corners, then turn the collar right side out and press again.

5. If your pattern does not have a back neck facing, the pattern instructions will tell you to press under the center of the ⅝-in. seam allowance of the upper collar. Trim the pressed-back seam allowance.

Machine-baste the collar to the garment along the neck edge, matching notches and dots. Also match the center of the collar to the center of the back neck.

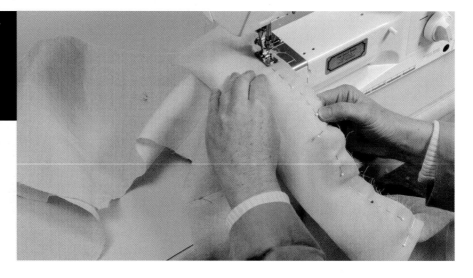

6. Machine-baste the collar in place along the neck edge of the shirt, matching notches and dots (see the bottom photo on the facing page). The collar will be permanently anchored in place when the facings are attached.

■ STAGE III: PUTTING IT ALL TOGETHER

The smaller puzzle pieces you have assembled all come together now, and the garment starts to take shape.

Attaching the facings

After the collar is attached, add the facings.

1. With right sides together, pin the facing to the front and neck edges (see the photo below).

2. Stitch directionally from the center of the back neck down each side, turning and sewing across the bottom edge of the facing.

3. Press the seam flat, then understitch the facing as far as you can by sewing both seam allowances to the facing, ⅛ in. from the attachment seam. Trim and grade the seams, and then press the facing to the wrong side, using a

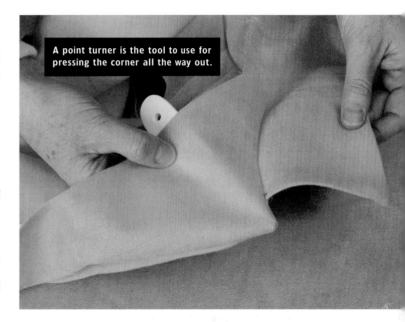

A point turner is the tool to use for pressing the corner all the way out.

Pin the facing to the front and neck edge.

point turner to press out the corner all the way (see the top photo on p. 135).

Hemming

Some of the best-made shirts and blouses have little rolled hems that are completed on the back and both front pieces before the side seams are sewn or the sleeves attached. Of course, the side seams are then French-seamed and no raw edges show, but hemming now is not out of order.

1. Begin by pressing up the hem after attaching the facing along the line of stitching that attached the facing in the hem area. Tuck under half of the hem and press again.

2. Topstitch the hem along the folded edge.

3. Press and stitch the hem edges of both front pieces and the back.

Alternately, you can make a tiny rolled hem.

1. Staystitch a line ¼ in. from the hem edge. Trim to ⅛ in.

2. Press up, then roll the hem up again and press (see the illustration below).

3. Stitch close to the folded edge. When you start stitching this rolled hem, hold the thread tails taut so that the fabric won't be pulled into the machine's throat plate. Keep pulling these threads until your stitching is under way. Hem the back and both front pieces the same way.

4. Press the finished hems.

Setting in sleeves

There are two basic ways to set in a shirt sleeve. The easiest way is to set the sleeve flat, attaching the sleeve before the side seams are sewn. Sometimes the sleeve shape is too curved to set in flat, so the fully constructed sleeve is sewn into the fully constructed shirt body. This is a sleeve set in the round. This second way is a little more difficult than the first but becomes easier once you get the hang of it. Both methods are described here.

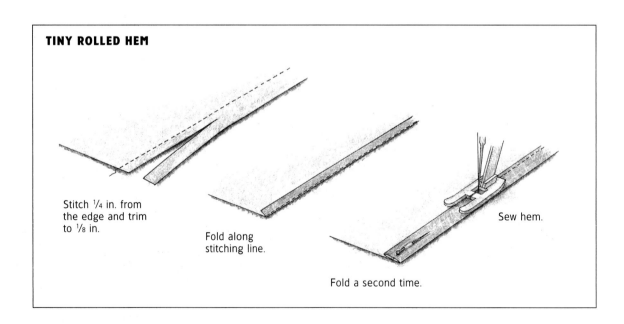

TINY ROLLED HEM

Stitch ¼ in. from the edge and trim to ⅛ in.

Fold along stitching line.

Fold a second time.

Sew hem.

SLEEVES SET IN FLAT The top of a shirt sleeve to be set in flat has a low curve. Regardless of the shape of the curve, you still need to ease this piece into the garment. The sleeves need shape and room to cover not only the arms but also the shoulders; it is easing at the top that makes a shape that fits the body.

1. Before setting in a sleeve, transfer all markings from the pattern to the fabric, including notches, dots, ease points, and the top of the sleeve. For notches and lines, snip the seam allowances ⅛ in.; for dots and shapes, use tailor tacks, chalk, or other markers. If the pattern has markings that indicate "ease between markings," be sure to mark them as well.

2. Using staystitch-plus (see "Staystitch-Plus" on p. 68), ease the top of the sleeve between notches or ease markings.

3. With right sides together, match the eased edge of the sleeve to the shirt armhole edge. Start by matching and pinning the center of the sleeve to the shoulder seams and working out in each direction. Note that double notches indicate the shirt back and a single notch indicates the shirt front; the sleeve will be similarly marked. The two pieces will not be flat against each other, but that is okay.

4. Sew the sleeve to the armhole edge using a ⅝-in. seam allowance. Because this is a curved seam that takes stress, sew the seam a second time right on top of the first line of stitching.

5. Next, trim the seam allowances to ¼ in. Zigzag or overlock the seam allowances together, then press toward the garment.

A shirt sleeve can be set flat, often with just a bit of easing. Match the top of the sleeve to the shoulder seam, the notches, and the ends. The pieces will not lie flat against each other, but the edges will match.

6. Hem the sleeve by pressing under ¼ in., and then pressing under another ¼ in. and top-stitching.

7. Finish the sleeve and the garment at the same time. Turn the garment so that right sides are together, then match and pin the underarm seam of the sleeve and the side seam of the garment. Sew using a ⅝-in. seam allowance.

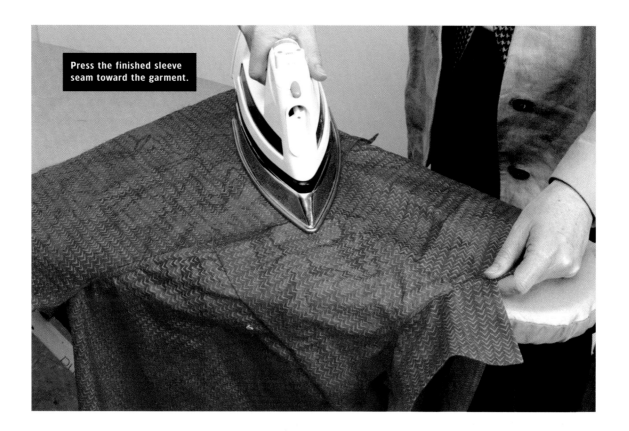

Press the finished sleeve seam toward the garment.

SLEEVES SET IN THE ROUND Classic blouse sleeves are set in the round. Before setting in the sleeves, stitch the underarm seam so that the sleeve becomes a tube. Also, sew the blouse front to the blouse back at the side seams.

1. Make sure that the notches and the center top of the sleeve are marked. If there are markings that indicate "ease between markings," mark them as well.

2. Using staystitch-plus (see "Staystitch-Plus" on p. 68), ease the top of the sleeve between notches or ease markings.

3. Working from the inside of the blouse, match the sleeve, which is right side out, to the armscye. Match the underarm seam of the sleeve to the side seam of the blouse, the snip

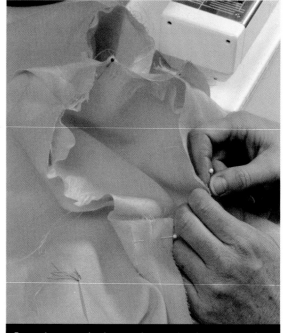

For a sleeve set in the round, ease the sleeve, then pin it to the garment, matching the top of the sleeve to the shoulder seams and notches.

CLASSIC SEAM FINISHES
FOR SHIRTS AND BLOUSES

There are two classic seam finishes for shirts and blouses: the flat-fell seam and the French seam. For instructions on how to construct a flat-fell seam, see p. 94. Here's how to construct a French seam.

1. For this technique, forget everything ever said about always sewing right sides together. Match and pin the seam allowance wrong sides together, then sew a ¼-in. seam.

2. Trim the seam allowance about ¹⁄₁₆ in. Don't press the seam allowance open; press it to one side, then fold the garment over the top of it. Press again, right along the seamline. Note that you are pressing with the garment pieces right sides together.

3. Pin and stitch ⅜ in. from the pressed edge (¼ in. + ⅜ in. = ⅝ in., the width of a standard seam allowance).

This seam finish is classically found in sheer fabrics, but I find that it is equally elegant for a not-quite-sheer fabric such as handkerchief linen. Regardless of fabric, though, it is a great way to finish the underarm and side seam of a blouse.

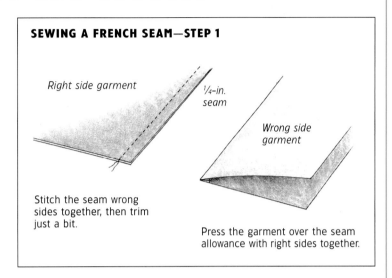

SEWING A FRENCH SEAM—STEP 1

Right side garment

¼-in. seam

Wrong side garment

Stitch the seam wrong sides together, then trim just a bit.

Press the garment over the seam allowance with right sides together.

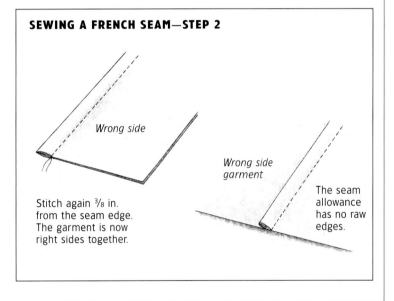

SEWING A FRENCH SEAM—STEP 2

Wrong side

Stitch again ⅜ in. from the seam edge. The garment is now right sides together.

Wrong side garment

The seam allowance has no raw edges.

at the top of the sleeve cap to the shoulder seam, and the notches on the front and back of the sleeve to those on the front and back of the blouse.

4. Sew the sleeve to the armhole edge using a ⅝-in. seam allowance. Because this is a curved seam that takes stress, make a second row of stitches right on top of the first.

5. Trim the seam allowances to ¼ in. Zigzag or overlock the seam allowances together, and press the sleeve toward the garment. After pressing, an optional finish is to topstitch

around the armhole, anchoring the seam allowances at the same time. Make sure you are topstitching on the garment side, not the sleeve side.

6. Hem the sleeve by pressing under ¼ in., and then pressing under another ¼ in. and topstitching.

■ STAGE IV: FINISHING

I no longer dread making buttonholes. Usually I'm so excited about being almost finished with my project that I just move right to the task.

Making buttonholes

The most important things to know about making buttonholes are knowing your machine, knowing how big to make the buttonhole, and knowing where to place and how to mark the buttonhole. After that, there are the tricks for making buttonholes and how to cut the buttonhole open.

KNOW YOUR MACHINE You need to know your machine to make a good buttonhole. Take out the manual and spend a couple of hours playing, reading, and trying to follow the directions. Or go to your sewing machine dealer and take lessons or ask the dealer to show you how to make a buttonhole.

What if the machine was your Great Aunt Mary's and you don't have the manual anymore? Go to a good sewing machine repair

Buttonholes and buttons are evenly spaced down from the breastbone. The top buttonhole and button can be placed where you want it above the breastbone at the neck.

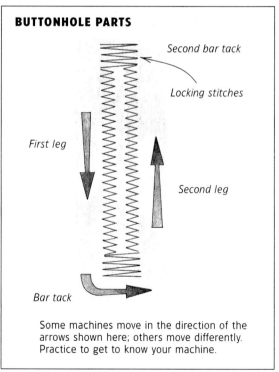

BUTTONHOLE PARTS

Second bar tack

Locking stitches

First leg

Second leg

Bar tack

Some machines move in the direction of the arrows shown here; others move differently. Practice to get to know your machine.

shop and ask the technician to show you. Offer to pay him, and take notes.

For the most part, the machine must include a zigzag feature and should have a special presser foot that is just for making buttonholes. A buttonhole puts a lot of thread in a small amount of space, and a regular presser foot cannot accommodate it all. The stitch length is shortened to almost 0, and some machines require special threading.

A machine-made buttonhole is divided into five parts: one leg of the buttonhole, which is made by the machine moving forward; a bar tack; the second leg of the buttonhole, which is made by the machine moving backward; the second bar tack; and then a few stitches to anchor the buttonhole (see the illustration on the facing page). Some machines automatically perform one or two of these steps in a row; then you tell it to go to the next step until you

are finished. Older machines may require you to dial each step. This is why you have to practice, so you know what your machine does and how and when you have to manipulate the dials and buttons.

KNOW HOW BIG TO MAKE THE BUTTONHOLES A buttonhole has to be big enough for the button to fit through but not so big that it floats around because then the garment won't stay closed.

1. To figure out how big to make a buttonhole, start by wrapping a strip of paper around one of the buttons you intend to use (see the photo below). Pinch the paper sharply so you can see a mark, then slide the button out.

2. Flatten the paper and measure from the fold to the mark (see the top photo on p. 142). This is the size buttonhole you need.

3. Always make a test buttonhole. Do this by making a sandwich of two layers of fabric with interfacing so you replicate the actual type and

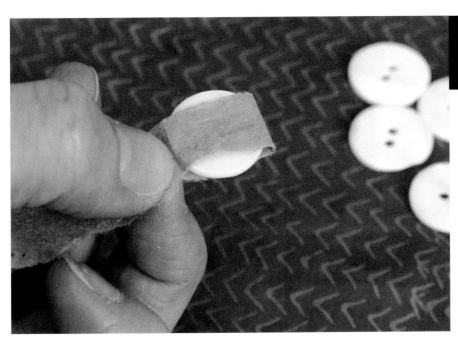

To measure a button for a buttonhole, wrap the button with a piece of paper and pinch it tightly.

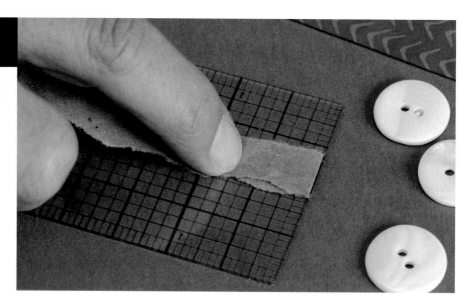

Flatten the paper and measure to the pinch mark.

Make a few test buttonholes on a "sandwich" of fabric plus interfacing plus fabric.

thickness of the fabric in the garment. Make a buttonhole the size you determined in step 2, then check to see that the button fits through it. If not, adjust the size and make another sample.

KNOW WHERE TO PLACE THE BUTTONHOLES Once you have determined the correct size buttonhole to make, it is time to mark the garment.

1. Leave a minimum distance between the front edge of the garment and the start of the

tip *Buttonholes on the front of ladies' garments go on the right.*

buttonhole that is half the diameter of the button plus ⅛ in.

2. Mark or make a line of basting stitches here, and mark the buttonholes in from this

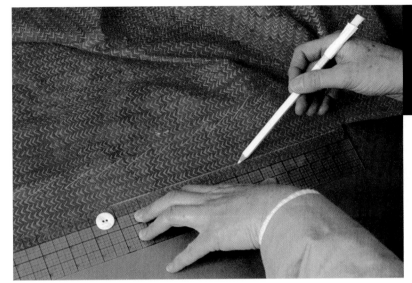

Establish your placement line for the buttonholes. The distance from the edge of the garment to the placement line should be a minimum of one-half the diameter of the button plus $1/8$ in. Mark the buttonholes in from the placement line.

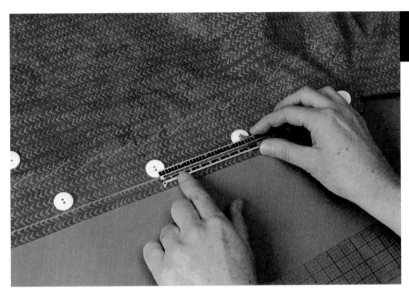

Measure from center to center to space the buttons. The top button does not have to be spaced evenly.

line. This is the starting line for stitching the buttonhole (see the top photo above).

3. If the buttons are the same size as the pattern recommends, space the buttonholes where the pattern indicates. Otherwise, experiment with placing the buttons until you have the spacing the way you want it. In general, mark the button placement at the breastbone first, then space the buttons evenly downward from there. The top buttonhole does not have to be equally spaced as the buttons below the breastbone.

4. Once you have determined the spacing, mark a horizontal line for each buttonhole, then mark each stopping line.

5. Make the buttonholes.

Mark the horizontal lines after you have determined the spacing.

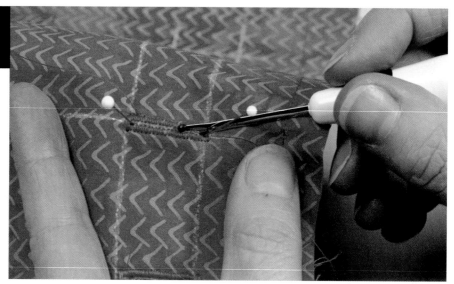

Place a pin at each end of the buttonhole before cutting it open with a sharp seam ripper.

tip *Mark buttonholes on the right side of the garment because you are going to sew on the right side. Use chalk, marking pens, or thread; if you use chalk or marking pens, first make sure that the marks will come off.*

6. Open the buttonholes. The best way to open up a buttonhole is with a buttonhole chisel. If you don't own this very sharp tool, place a pin at each end of the buttonhole. Use a sharp seam ripper to start the cut (see the bottom photo above), then work toward each pin with the seam ripper or with small, sharp scissors.

Here are some helpful pointers for making buttonholes.

• Sometimes it is possible to change the look of the buttonhole stitches while you are sewing. My older machine allows me to adjust the stitch length for the second, backward leg of the buttonhole by shortening the stitch length when I start this leg. However, when I do this on the electronic machines at The Sewing Workshop, I interfere with the programmed buttonhole stitch and really mess things up. Read the manual and practice—you may be able to adjust as you go, you may not.

• A corded buttonhole (where the stitches on each leg wrap over a thick thread) is not much harder to make than a regular buttonhole, and in some fabrics it is the only way to make the buttonhole show up. Read the manual or ask your dealer or repair person if your machine can do this.

• Before cutting buttonholes open, a dressmaker I know bathes her buttonholes with Fray Check, which is the sewer's equivalent to clear nail polish. It keeps buttonholes from unraveling if you accidentally cut the threads. Beware, though, that the color in some fabrics runs (I speak from experi-ence). Test the Fray Check on a scrap before you use it on your garment.

• You can take a permanent felt pen and color the light interfacing so that it doesn't show in your dark fabric garments. After coloring the interfacing, rub Fray Check on the edges so the color doesn't come off.

• I was taught to make button-holes from the bottom of the gar-ment to the top. This is so the top buttonhole —the one that shows the most—would be the best looking. Don't believe it! On a blouse or shirt, buried beneath the very spot where the top-most buttonhole will go, are more overlapping seam allowances than anywhere else on the garment. The presser foot may want to slide to one side or the other (it seeks the flattest spot of its own free will), and you will be struggling to get this buttonhole in. Sometimes just being aware of this makes it easier to make the buttonhole. Better still, knowing there might be a problem in advance allows you the opportunity to get in there before making the buttonhole and trimming the seam allowances so they are as much out of the way as possible.

A corded buttonhole is a buttonhole worked over a thicker piece of thread, which helps the buttonhole stand out, especially in bulky fabric.

Sewing on buttons

Most people know how to sew on a button, but there are some tricks for making it easy.

1. Thread a needle with double thread so there are four threads on the needle. Knot the end of the thread.

2. Overlap and pin the garment fronts. Stick a pin through the buttonhole close to the center front edge of the garment, then slip the but-tonhole off over the pin. The pin becomes the mark for your button.

Overlap the shirt fronts and place a pin through the edge of the button-hole closest to the center front. This is where the button goes.

Wrap the threads between the button and the garment to help the button stand up.

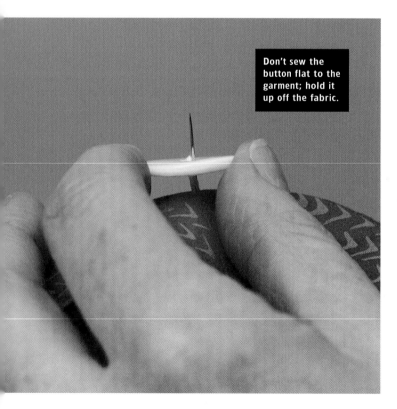

Don't sew the button flat to the garment; hold it up off the fabric.

3. When you sew the button, hold it up off the fabric, as shown in the bottom photo at left. (In the old days, we were instructed to put a matchstick under the button to hold it up.) Sewing with four threads allows you to attach the button with only a couple of stitches.

4. After the button feels secure, bring your needle up between the fabric and the button. Wrap the thread around the threads under the button. Bring the needle down to the wrong side of the garment to knot off.

■ ADDING ON

For a first shirt or blouse project, stick with the basics. Add on as your confidence and skills grow. Before too long, any shirt or blouse—

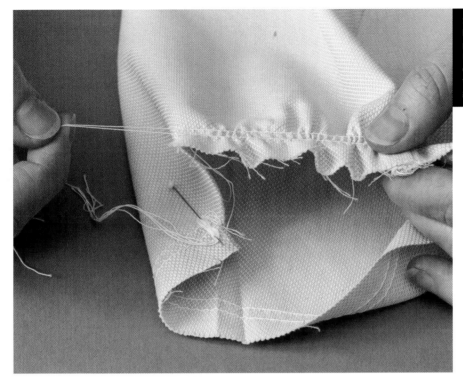

Sleeves are gathered by making two rows of parallel basting stitches. Pin the thread tails on one side, then pull the threads together to gather.

topstitched, buttonholed, two-piece collared, long sleeved, and yoked—will be part of your sewing repertoire.

If your shirt pattern has a long sleeve and will be set in the round (see pp. 138–140), finish the cuff and the opening above the cuff, called the placket, before setting the sleeve.

Constructing a long sleeve with a cuff

The bottom edge of a long sleeve can be gathered or pleated into a cuff, which can be constructed in a variety of ways, sometimes with an opening called a sleeve placket. Then the sleeve placket has to be finished.

GATHERING THE SLEEVE EDGE

1. Make sure that all markings for the bottom of the sleeve have been transferred from the pattern to the fabric. For gathers, the pattern may have dots or lines or instructions to "ease between" certain marks.

2. To gather a sleeve edge, make two parallel rows of machine-basting where indicated by the pattern.

3. Pin all of the threads at one end and pull the top two threads at the other until the sleeve edge matches the cuff in length (see the photo above).

PLEATING THE SLEEVE EDGE

1. Make sure all markings for the bottom of the sleeve have been transferred from the pattern to the fabric. Pleats have distinctive markings: lines, arrows, or Xs indicate foldlines, matchlines, and pleat direction.

2. Pinch the fabric along the foldline and bring the fold to the second line, or placement

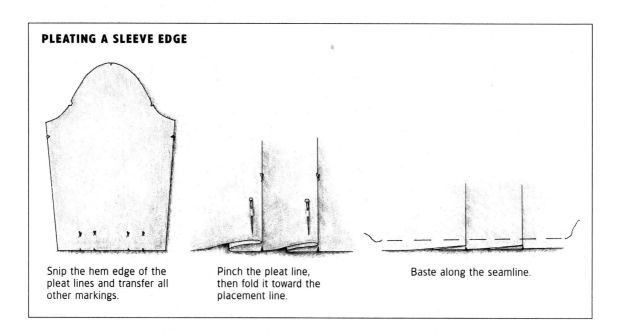

PLEATING A SLEEVE EDGE

Snip the hem edge of the pleat lines and transfer all other markings.

Pinch the pleat line, then fold it toward the placement line.

Baste along the seamline.

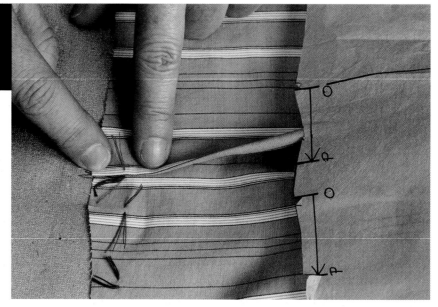

To pleat a sleeve edge, pinch the foldline and place it on top of the placement line, following the direction of the arrows on the pattern piece.

line, following the direction of the arrow on the pattern. Pin (see the photo above).

3. Fold and pin all pleats, and then anchor them with hand-basting or machine-basting about ½ in. from the edge of the sleeve.

MAKING A BASIC SLEEVE PLACKET The sleeve opening above the cuff on a long sleeve is finished after the bottom edge of the sleeve is pleated or gathered and before the seam is sewn and the cuff attached.

1. Look at the pattern to see if the placket opening appears as a dart shape or a line. If there is a dart shape, staystitch along the outline of the shape. If there is a line, stitch ¼ in.

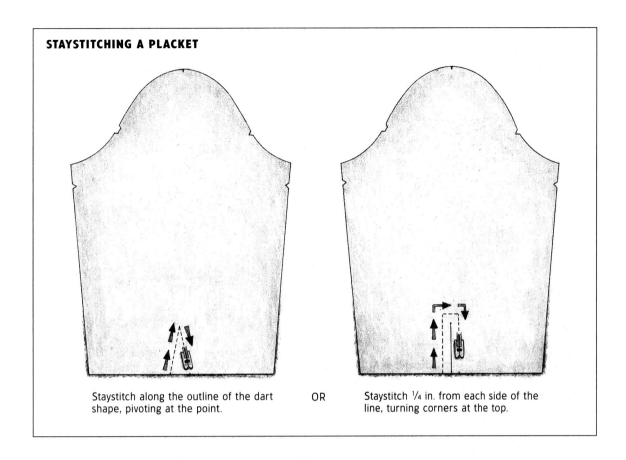

STAYSTITCHING A PLACKET

Staystitch along the outline of the dart shape, pivoting at the point.

OR

Staystitch ¼ in. from each side of the line, turning corners at the top.

from the line, pivot at the top of the line, sew across four or five stitches, then pivot and sew along the other side of the line ¼ in. away (see the illustration above).

2. After staystitching the dart shape, slash along the center line to the dart point. Alternatively, after staystitching along both sides of the line, slash along the line to ¼ in. from the top, and then snip to but not through each corner of the staystitching (see the photo at right).

3. With right sides together, pin the binding or placket piece to the entire length of the opening, pinning the center as well as both ends and midpoints (see the photo at left on p. 150).

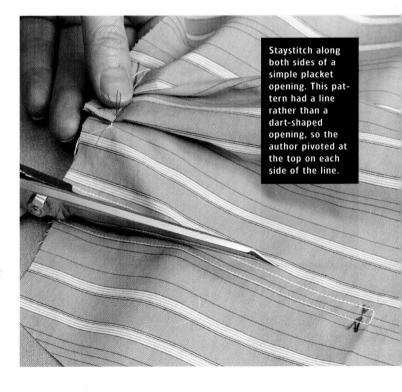

Staystitch along both sides of a simple placket opening. This pattern had a line rather than a dart-shaped opening, so the author pivoted at the top on each side of the line.

Match the placket piece or binding piece along the entire opening. Pin at the first corner or at the top of the dart and sew to that point.

Once you reach the first corner or the top of the dart, put the needle down in the fabric and lift the presser foot. Move all of the fabric to the left side and back of the machine, then put the presser foot down and resume sewing.

4. Sew the strip to the sleeve opening (see the left photo above), stopping at the midpoint with the needle down or hand turning the fly wheel to move the needle down. Lift the presser foot, pivot the garment, and smooth out the fabric so that it will not be caught up in the next half of the stitching. Put the presser foot down and continue to the edge of the sleeve (see the photo at right above). If the sleeve has a dart-shaped placket opening, the edges of the strip should not match the edge of the opening. Instead, the edge of the strip should be an even ¼ in. above the line of stitching.

5. Press the strip toward the seam allowance. Looking at the wrong side of the strip, press the edge of the strip in to meet the seam allowance, then press it in half over the stitching line (see the photo at left on the facing page). Pin.

6. Topstitch the strip in place close to the attachment seam, then press.

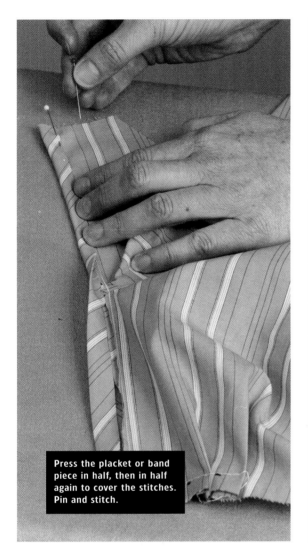

Press the placket or band piece in half, then in half again to cover the stitches. Pin and stitch.

On the wrong side of the garment, sew diagonally across the folded placket. Here, I've pinned right where I'm going to sew.

7. Turn the sleeve inside out. Match the two edges of the placket opening, then stitch diagonally across the small edge at the top of the placket (see the photo at right above).

MAKING A BASIC OPENING From time to time, you will come across a pattern with a sleeve opening that has no placket. The opening on this type of sleeve is the distance between one edge of the cuff and the other. When the edges of the cuff are overlapped and buttoned, the opening doesn't show.

1. Begin by making sure that you have transferred all markings from the pattern to the sleeve.

2. Staystitch the edge of the opening and clip to the staystitching at each end (see the top illustration on p. 152). Turn under and press the opening in half toward the staystitching. Turn and press again, then pin along the folded edge. Stitch through the folded edges, much like making a narrow hem (see p. 136). Hold the tails of the threads taut as you begin stitching

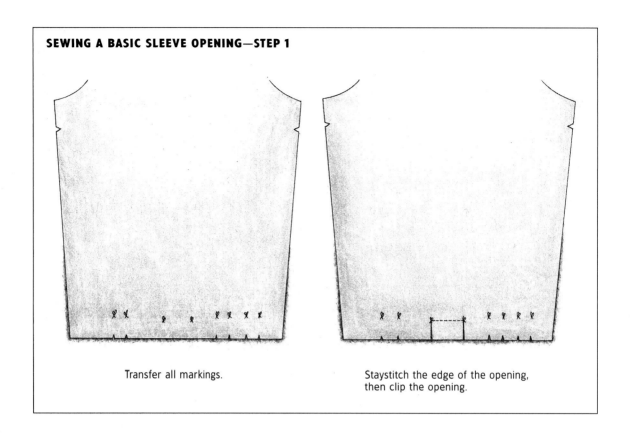

SEWING A BASIC SLEEVE OPENING—STEP 1

Transfer all markings.

Staystitch the edge of the opening, then clip the opening.

to prevent the narrow edge from being pulled under the feed dogs.

MAKING A BASIC CUFF Cuffs are similar in construction to collars. The easiest construction is a single cuff piece that is folded in half to form the cuff.

1. Interface the cuff following the instructions for interfacing the collar on pp. 123–124. Press under ⅝ in. of the unnotched edge of the cuff.

2. Match and pin the right side of the cuff to the right side of the sleeve edge. Stitch using a ⅝-in. seam allowance, starting and stopping ⅝ in. from each edge. Trim the seam allowance if it is bulky, and press the cuff and both seam allowances away from the sleeve (see the top photo on the facing page).

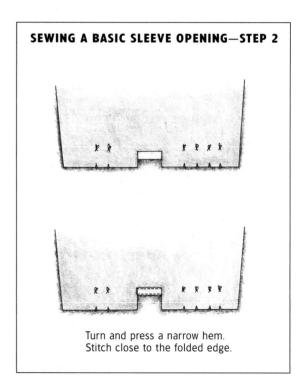

SEWING A BASIC SLEEVE OPENING—STEP 2

Turn and press a narrow hem.
Stitch close to the folded edge.

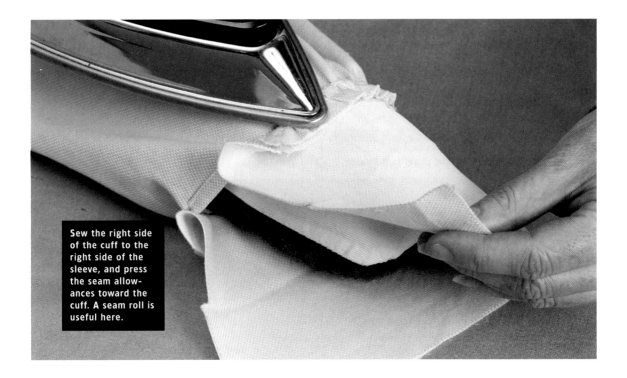

Sew the right side of the cuff to the right side of the sleeve, and press the seam allowances toward the cuff. A seam roll is useful here.

3. With right sides together, fold the cuff in half along the foldline, then press. Pin and stitch each short edge, catching the folded-back seam allowance but not catching any of the sleeve.

4. Press the seams open (use a tailor board if you have one), and then trim the seam allowances. Turn the cuff right side out, pushing out the corners with a point turner. Tuck in the seam allowance and press again.

5. Finish the sleeve by topstitching through all thicknesses along the folded-under edge of the cuff.

MAKING TWO-PIECE CUFFS A two-piece cuff is constructed with an upper cuff piece and an under cuff piece.

1. Start by interfacing one or both cuff pieces. If you interface only one, that piece should be the upper cuff. Otherwise, designate one piece

Stitch across the short ends, catching the folded-back seam allowance.

The upper yoke is attached to the shirt back.

After the yoke is attached to the shirt back and fronts, roll up the back so that you can see the seam allowance that attaches the yoke.

5. Roll up the shirt fronts toward the neck edge until the yoke seam allowances show (see the top photo on the facing page).

6. Match and pin the under yoke fronts to this seam allowance with right sides together (see the bottom left photo on the facing page). Sew the seams over the previous stitching.

7. Turn the shirt right side out by pulling it through the neck opening (see the bottom right photo on the facing page).

8. Press the yoke, then attach the collar and facings.

Roll up each front so that you can see the seam allowances.

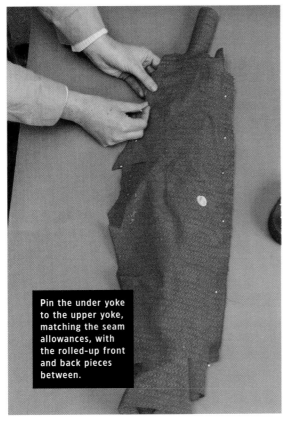

Pin the under yoke to the upper yoke, matching the seam allowances, with the rolled-up front and back pieces between.

To finish, pull the front and back pieces out through the neck edge.

easy jackets

■ ■ 5 ■

I made my first jacket when I was 15 or 16. All the girls in my Girl Scout Roundup patrol made gold jackets, although I think most of the moms did the sewing. My jacket didn't look as nice as the ones made by the moms, but it didn't look too bad. The fabric was cotton, and the pattern had a hood and a separating zipper rather than buttons and buttonholes. I made that jacket again a year later in a burgundy cotton. But the second time I made it, I lined the jacket with pink gingham, and I did a much better job.

Pattern: Vogue
1827
Fabric: Rayon
Needle: 80/12 H
Thread: Mettler
silk-finish cotton
Straight stitch, 2.5

Stage 1: Project preparation
- Buy the pattern and test it in muslin or scrap fabric.
- Check and alter fit as needed.
- Buy the fabric and notions, including shoulder pads.
- Buy interfacing.
- Prepare the fabric (see Chapter 1 beginning on p. 2).

Stage 2: Getting under way
- Cut and mark the fabric.
- Staystitch the front and back neck edges.
- Cut the back stay and finish its bottom edge.
- Interface the front and back neck facings, sleeve hems, and jacket hem.

- Overlock or serge the seam edges, if desired.

Stage 3: Time to sew!
- Sew the darts or princess seams and the center back seam.
- Baste the back stay in place along the back neck edge, shoulders, armholes, and sides.
- Stay the neck edge.
- Attach a lined patch pocket with a foldback facing.
- Sew the back to the front at the shoulder seams, inserting twill tape in the seams to stabilize them.
- Sew the back neck facing to the front neck facing.
- Prepare the collar.

- Apply facing to the jacket and press.
- Attach the side-seam pockets, if any.
- Sew the side seams.
- Finish and insert the sleeves, using a bias strip to ease the sleeve cap.
- Sew in the half-lining or full facing.
- Cover the armhole seam with bias binding.

Stage 4: Finishing
- Cover and insert the shoulder pads.
- Hem the jacket.
- Make the buttonholes and attach the buttons.

I love to make jackets, so I always have at least one ongoing jacket project. Making a jacket requires planning, dividing the project into doable sections, attending to details such as interfacing, choosing a pocket style, attaching collars and facings, and finishing seams. Jackets are important wardrobe pieces. They deserve a lot of attention when we're making them, and because we give them that attention, they last a long time.

There is a good deal of important jacket-making information that isn't found in pattern instructions. This chapter is about filling in the blanks—about the important information and techniques you need to successfully complete an easy jacket.

Let's start at the beginning: If you want to make an easy jacket, you need to choose an easy pattern. Limit your pattern choices to jackets without collars—those with jewel or V necklines—and avoid patterns with many pieces and details that would take longer to construct.

If you organize your sewing project into small steps, you'll find you can successfully make a jacket. I organize my jacket projects into four basic steps: project preparation, which includes pattern work and fabric preparation; cutting, marking, and interfacing; sewing; and finishing. Here's how these steps work in the construction sequence.

■ STAGE I: PROJECT PREPARATION

Spend some time at the fabric store looking at patterns and fabrics and thinking about the project before you buy anything. You are going to be spending a lot of time on this project and will want to be sure that you like what you've chosen.

Buying the pattern

Look on the pattern envelope for the line drawings that show the jacket's design, shape, and construction details. These drawings will help you determine how difficult the jacket will be to sew. Here are a few suggestions. A jacket with a center back seam has fewer pattern pieces and is easier to sew than one with princess seams, while still giving you a seamline to alter and shape. Front and side bust darts prevent a jacket from looking boxy and are also easier to construct than princess seams. A two-piece jacket sleeve has a little more shaping and a slightly better fit than a one-piece sleeve. Although welt pockets are beautiful details for a tailored jacket, patch and in-seam pockets are much simpler and faster to construct and are always my choices for an easy jacket. I like to play around with patch pockets, making them oversized or changing the shape or placement.

To avoid a homemade look, stay away from patterns with necklines that are too wide (they won't fit well); those with sleeves cut as part of the front and back (you'll have too much fabric under the arms at the bustline); and those with boxy bodies (you'll look, well, boxy). Although a jacket with set-in sleeves is more difficult to construct than a raglan or dolman sleeve jacket, it's also more flattering. If you're really a beginner, you can choose a pattern with slightly dropped sleeves, which are easier to construct.

Your pattern will instruct you to line the jacket or to construct an unlined one. If you don't fully line the jacket, alternative but relatively easy inside finishes include fully facing or half-lining the jacket. Both add a more finished look to the inside of the garment and eliminate the need for seam finishes on the side and shoulder seams.

Testing your pattern in muslin or scrap fabric

Just as you would before you purchase any new pattern, take your measurements and compare them to the pattern you have chosen. Alter the pattern where necessary. Project preparation includes making a test garment in muslin or scrap fabric. I know this sounds anything but easy, but you are going to put a lot of work into this jacket. You need to know before you finish whether the pattern fits or can be altered and whether it is flattering.

Making a muslin is fast: Cut out the fronts, backs, and sleeves. If your pattern has a collar, you can leave it out. Also leave out the facings and pockets. Using a tracing wheel and tracing paper, transfer the dart markings, the center front, and the waistline. Sew the jacket "fast and dirty," being sure to put in both sleeves.

> **tip** *Scrap fabric doesn't mean an old sheet. Sheets are tightly woven and difficult to sew—who needs that! A scrap piece of flannel or cotton is what you are looking for.*

Checking and altering fit as needed

When you try on the muslin, trust your judgment: If the jacket doesn't look good in muslin, chances are it won't in expensive fashion fabric. What are you looking for? Pin the jacket fronts together at the center front line. Is the jacket too long or too short? This is an easy alteration. Does the jacket fit in the waist and hip areas? Once again, easy to alter. Is the shoulder line along your shoulder? If it keeps pulling to the back, you can adjust the balance. Where does the neckline lie? Remember that the ⅝-in. seam allowances will be turned under to the wrong side. Lift up your arm—is the armhole high enough to allow easy movement? I've rejected patterns with bad sleeves and necklines, but if the sleeve is just too tight across the bicep, you can alter the sleeve pattern fairly easily and adjust the sleeve length, too.

LENGTH The first alteration that should be made is lengthening or shortening the pattern. If the alteration needed is 1 in. or less, simply add to or subtract from the hem edge. If you need to add or subtract more, divide the alteration by two and add or subtract half above the waist and half below the waist. To shorten, slash the pattern along the lengthen/shorten lines and overlap the desired amount. To lengthen, slash the pattern and spread it apart the desired amount, then tape a piece of tissue paper between the slashes (see the illustration below).

WIDTH Waist and hip alterations are among the easiest to make. Divide the amount you need to add by four (because there are four sides: right side front and right side back, left side

---

ADJUSTING THE LENGTH

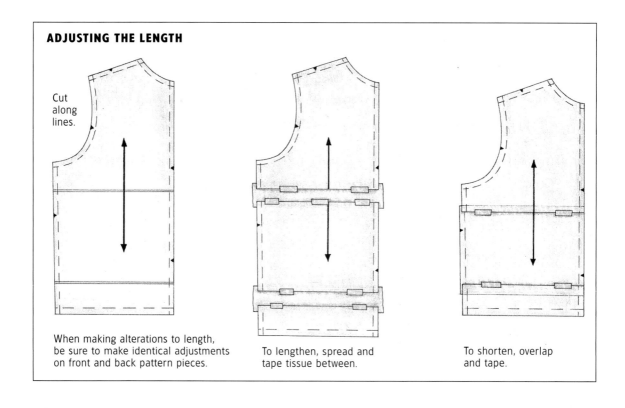

Cut along lines.

When making alterations to length, be sure to make identical adjustments on front and back pattern pieces.

To lengthen, spread and tape tissue between.

To shorten, overlap and tape.

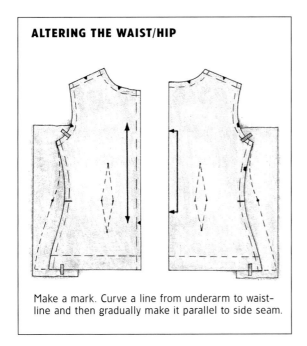

ALTERING THE WAIST/HIP

Make a mark. Curve a line from underarm to waist-line and then gradually make it parallel to side seam.

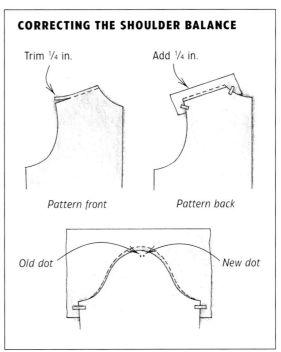

CORRECTING THE SHOULDER BALANCE

Trim ¼ in.

Add ¼ in.

Pattern front

Pattern back

Old dot

New dot

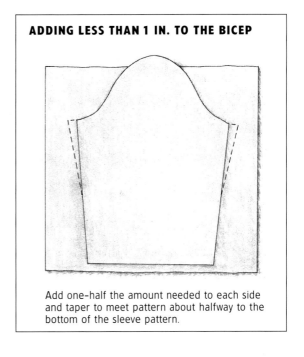

ADDING LESS THAN 1 IN. TO THE BICEP

Add one-half the amount needed to each side and taper to meet pattern about halfway to the bottom of the sleeve pattern.

front and left side back), and then add this amount to each side. Make a mark the amount you want to add adjacent to the waist or hip on the side fronts and side backs. Using a curved ruler (or just eyeballing it), draw a line connecting the underarm to the new mark. Continue the line to the hem of the garment, but keep the line an even distance from the edge of the pattern all the way to the hem.

SHOULDER BALANCE If the muslin jacket you made shifts to the back at the shoulder, the alteration is easy to make. To correct shoulder balance, the basic alteration is to subtract ¼ in. from the front shoulder seams and to add ¼ in. to the back shoulder seams. This puts more fabric in the garment back where it needs it. If you make this alteration, move the dot on the top of the sleeve cap ¼ in. toward the front.

SLEEVE WIDTH Jacket sleeves can be a problem because many of them are poorly designed. A jacket sleeve in the upper arm area needs to be 3 in. to 4 in. bigger than the bicep to provide the correct amount of ease. If you need to add 1 in. or less, follow the instructions on p. 168.

The sleeve needs to be bigger than the garment hole it is sewn into so that there is room for your arm. It needs to be bigger by up to 2 in. (but no more than that).

1. Place the sleeve pattern on a larger piece of paper.

2. Divide the amount you need to add to the pattern in half. Make a dot that distance away from the top of the sleeve seam on each side.

3. Extend the curve of the sleeve cap out to meet the new mark, and taper the new mark into the existing seams about halfway down the sleeve. The extra fabric you have added will be eased into the armscye.

To add more than 1 in. requires more work.

1. Draw a line down the center of the sleeve and cut the pattern apart. Place a strip of tissue paper under the spread-out pattern pieces and pin or tape together.

2. After adding the strip of paper, adjust the sleeve cap so that it will fit in the armscye. To do this, measure the new sleeve curve along the seamline from side seam to side seam, excluding seam allowances. Then measure the armscye, which is the combined length of the armhole edges on the jacket front and jacket back, excluding seam allowances. (Think of this as the garment armhole.)

If the sleeve is more than 2 in. larger than the armscye, make a slash down the center of the new sleeve (the one with the added paper). Cut almost to the bottom edge but not through it.

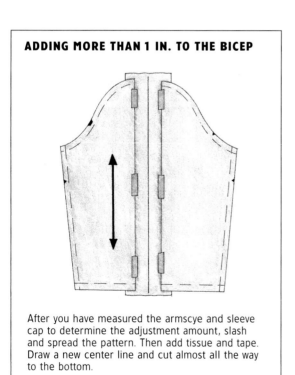

ADDING MORE THAN 1 IN. TO THE BICEP

After you have measured the armscye and sleeve cap to determine the adjustment amount, slash and spread the pattern. Then add tissue and tape. Draw a new center line and cut almost all the way to the bottom.

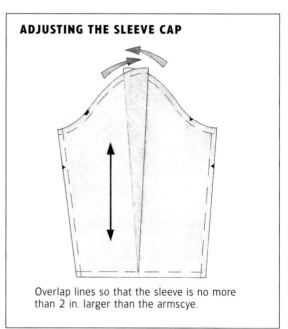

ADJUSTING THE SLEEVE CAP

Overlap lines so that the sleeve is no more than 2 in. larger than the armscye.

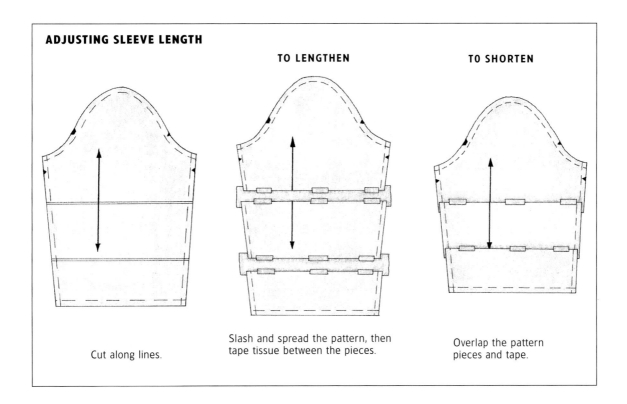

ADJUSTING SLEEVE LENGTH

TO LENGTHEN

TO SHORTEN

Cut along lines.

Slash and spread the pattern, then tape tissue between the pieces.

Overlap the pattern pieces and tape.

3. Pivot the two halves of the sleeve toward each other, overlapping them at the cap of the sleeve, until the cap of the sleeve is no more than 2 in. larger than the armscye (see the illustration at right on the facing page).

SLEEVE LENGTH Sleeve length is added in the same way as garment length. If the alteration needed is 1 in. or less, simply add to or subtract from the sleeve hem edge. If you need to add or subtract more, divide the alteration by two and add or subtract half above the elbow and half below the elbow. To shorten, slash the pattern along the lengthen/shorten lines and overlap the desired amount. To lengthen, slash the pattern and spread it apart the desired amount, and then tape a piece of tissue paper between the slashes. Redraw seamlines after you have made the adjustment.

Buying fabric and notions

Once you've settled on a pattern, you're ready to buy fabric. For a first jacket, consider a medium-weight, even-textured linen or a tweedy or knubby wool or wool blend. Linen is easy to work with but is seasonal. Wools are easy to work with, too. And tweedy and knubby fabrics hide sewing imperfections. Fabrics to avoid for jackets include polyester or polyester blends, since they resist pressing and shaping, and wool gabardine, which requires advanced pressing and topstitching skills. Others I would steer clear of are flimsy and lightweight fabrics, which make better shirts than jackets, and fabrics with very smooth surfaces, since every detail will show. When you buy fabric, also buy whatever notions are listed on the pattern envelope.

Buying interfacing

While you are at the fabric store, there are a couple of other supplies you'll need besides thread to match your fashion fabric and buttons. Jackets need what I call substructure so that they will last. There are five essential places to add substructure to a jacket. First, the shoulder seams need to be stabilized with twill tape

> **tip** *Except for interfacing the hems, all of the areas I recommend stabilizing are at the top of the jacket where the pieces come together—the shoulders and sleeves and the front and back neck edges. For an easy jacket, I suggest using a minimum amount of interfacing. More tailored jackets require much more interfacing.*

or linen stay tape (sometimes referred to as tailor's tape). Second, the back needs the addition of a back stay, which is a shaped piece of lining fabric that is attached to the upper back. Third, the front and back neck facings need to be interfaced, as does the collar if the pattern has one. Fourth, the sleeves require a strip of interfacing to ease and support them. And fifth, the hems need to be interfaced.

Fusible interfacing is recommended for easy jackets. There is a wide variety of fusible interfacings available, but my favorites are Fusi-Knit and Sof Knit, as well as Armo weft for wools. Some interfacings are softer than others, some are stiffer. If the interfacing available at your fabric store seems cardboardy, chances are it will make your fabric look that way, too. Check Resources on p. 214 for places where good interfacing is available. When you start using good fusible interfacings, you will notice

Jackets need interfacing at the shoulders, along the neck edges, at the back, at the top of the sleeves, and in the hems. Shown from left: fusible interfacing, back stay cut from lining fabric, bias tape, linen stay tape, twill tape, bias strips to ease the shoulders, fusible interfacing for the hem, and shoulder pads.

how much better they are than mediocre ones and what a difference they make in the way your garments look.

Purchase enough interfacing for the front facings, back neck facings, and the garment and sleeve hems.

■ STAGE II: GETTING UNDER WAY

The next stage in constructing a jacket includes cutting and marking the fashion fabric; staystitching the neck edges; cutting the back stay and finishing its bottom edge; and interfacing the facings and hems. Do these steps carefully and you'll be pleased with the results.

Cutting and marking the fashion fabric

Lay out the fabric according to the pattern instructions and pin, checking that the grainlines are straight as you go. Cut out each pattern piece, and then mark the notches with small snips and mark the darts, the top of the sleeve, and all other dots, squares, triangles, and circles using tailor tacks, chalk, or other markers. If the jacket has pockets, mark the pocket placement line (sometimes it's just one corner that's marked).

Staystitching the front and back neck edges

Because the pieces are still unassembled, it's easy to staystitch the front and back neck edges now. After winding a bobbin with thread that matches your fashion fabric, sew through one layer of fabric a little bit less than ⅝ in. from the neck edge (see "Staystitching" on p. 90).

A collarless jacket with a V-neckline is a good choice for a first jacket project.

Cutting the back stay and finishing its bottom edge

To cut the back stay, you will have to make the pattern yourself. Using the pattern back piece, make a mark 2 in. below the armhole on the side seam (see the illustration on p. 172). On the center back seam (or center back line if there is no seam), make another mark about 2 in. above the side seam mark. Draw a curved line from the mark on the center back to the mark on the side seam below the armhole. Curve the line out, then down and out to the side seam mark. Curving the edge allows you to reach and move inside your jacket.

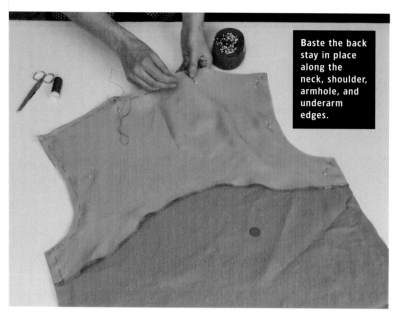

Baste the back stay in place along the neck, shoulder, armhole, and underarm edges.

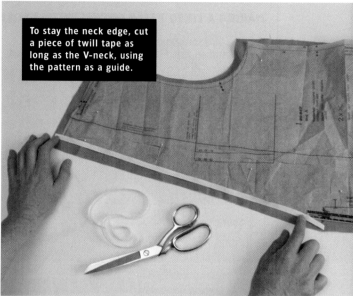

To stay the neck edge, cut a piece of twill tape as long as the V-neck, using the pattern as a guide.

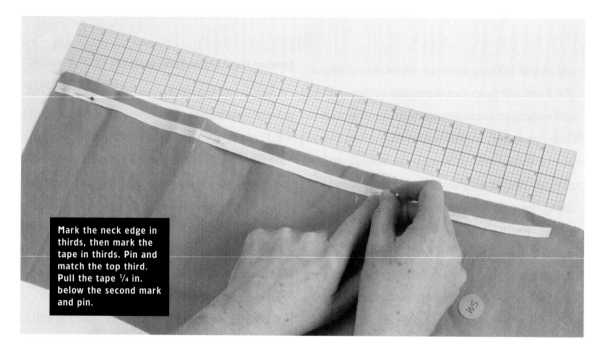

Mark the neck edge in thirds, then mark the tape in thirds. Pin and match the top third. Pull the tape 1/4 in. below the second mark and pin.

end of the V. Cut two pieces of stay tape, one for each side of the jacket front.

2. On the wrong side of the jacket front, pin the tape from the shoulder down along the seam allowance about one-third the distance. Mark the second one-third on the jacket and

on the stay tape, and then pin the marked stay tape 1/4 in. below the mark on the jacket. Pin the rest of the stay tape.

3. Stitch the tape to the garment at just about the 5/8-in. seam allowance. Be sure to sew with

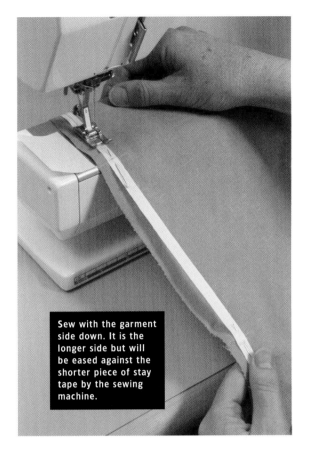

Sew with the garment side down. It is the longer side but will be eased against the shorter piece of stay tape by the sewing machine.

the garment side down so that the tape is eased into place (see the photo at left).

Sewing the shoulder seams

To sew the shoulder seams, place the garment back right side up on a flat surface, and then place each garment front piece right side down on the garment back, matching the pieces along the shoulder seams.

You may notice that the neck edges aren't curved the same. The difference in shape doesn't matter; it is only necessary to match the pieces along the ⅝-in. seam allowance line. Pin the pieces together.

Using the pattern as a guide, cut two pieces of linen stay tape or twill tape the length of the shoulder seams. Next, with the garment fronts up, place the tape along the seamline, centering it along the seam allowance, and repin. Stitch

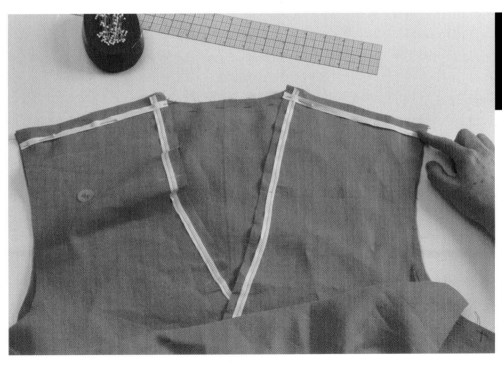

A V-neck jacket is stayed along the neck edge and at the shoulder seams.

through all layers, backstitching at the beginning and end of the seamline, and then press the seam allowances open.

Sewing the jacket facings

Attaching the facings to the jacket is an important step in jacket-making. The garment will really look like a jacket when finished.

1. Begin by sewing the back neck facing to the front neck facings at the shoulder seams and pressing the seams open.

2. With right sides together, place the combined back neck facing/front neck facing on the neck edge of the jacket. (If the jacket has an easy collar, the collar will be sandwiched between these layers.) Pin so that you can sew directionally from the center back seam down to the hem on one side and from the center back seam down to the hem on the second side. Lengthen the stitch on your sewing machine if the layers are thick.

3. Sew from the center back neck to the hem on each side of the jacket, and then press the seam flat.

4. Working on the edge of the ironing board or on a June Tailor board, press the seams open. Then trim the seam allowances, grading them so that the seam allowance that is closest to the top of the garment is slightly wider than the seam allowance closest to the facing. This will eliminate bulk and help the facing lie flat.

5. Tailor-baste along the neck edge to the hem. Use silk thread (if you have it) that is double threaded on a needle but left unknot-

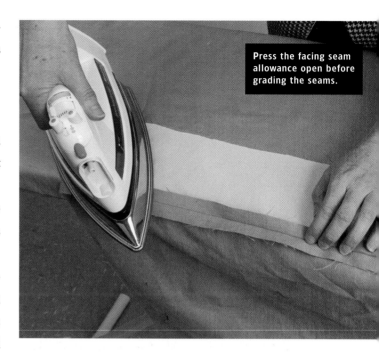

Press the facing seam allowance open before grading the seams.

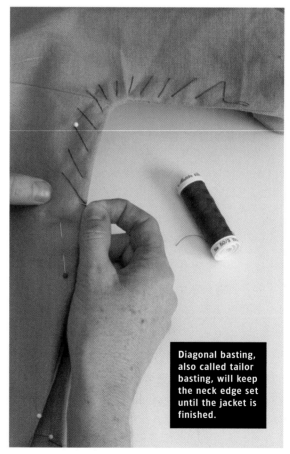

Diagonal basting, also called tailor basting, will keep the neck edge set until the jacket is finished.

ted. Start at the center back neck edge. Take a stitch to start, then take a backstitch. Begin tailor basting: Put your needle in close to the neck edge and draw the thread ¾ in. to 1 in. straight out from the edge; return to the neck edge. Continue to stitch like this—in at the neck edge, then the needle out 1 in. away from the neck edge. Your stitches will look like diagonal lines on the right side of the garment (see the bottom photo on the facing page). As you are working, push the facing toward the inside of the garment with your fingers. The basting will help set the shape of the neck and front edges of the jacket.

6. Finally, press. If you have used silk thread, you can press without leaving the thread impressions that cotton or polyester thread would leave. Leave the basting in place until you have finished the jacket.

Sewing side-seam pockets and side seams

If you are not inserting side-seam pockets, sew the side seams together before setting the sleeves.

Although jackets normally have patch or inset pockets, you can substitute a pocket in the side seam by using the pocket placement line as your guide. Start by marking the garment side seams to indicate where the top of the pocket will be, then follow these steps.

1. Using the rectangular patch pocket piece or a shaped side-seam pocket piece from another garment, pin each pocket piece to the side seam of the front and back garment pieces. Use the markings you have made on the side seams as placement guides.

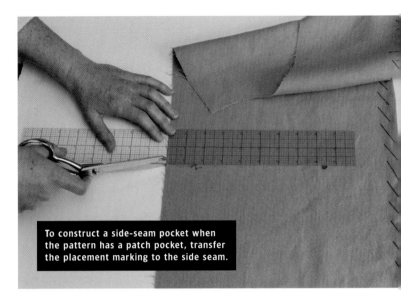

To construct a side-seam pocket when the pattern has a patch pocket, transfer the placement marking to the side seam.

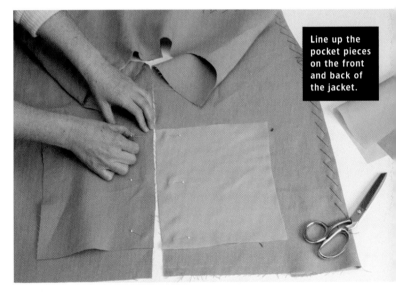

Line up the pocket pieces on the front and back of the jacket.

2. Sew each pocket piece in place using a ⅜-in. seam allowance.

3. Press the pocket pieces to the side of the garment.

4. Next, place the front garment pieces right sides together on the back garment piece. Using a ⅝-in. seam allowance, sew the side seams to approximately 1½ in. below the top of

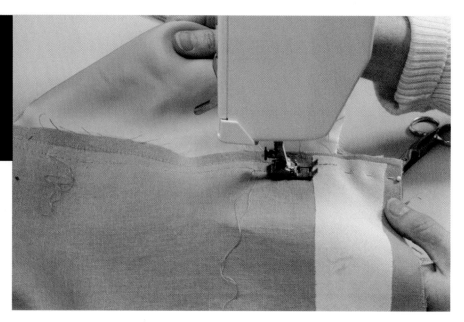

After attaching pocket pieces with a ³/₈-in. seam allowance, sew the side seams, basting across the pocket opening. Leave thread tails between the regular stitching and the basting stitches so you can remove the basting easily.

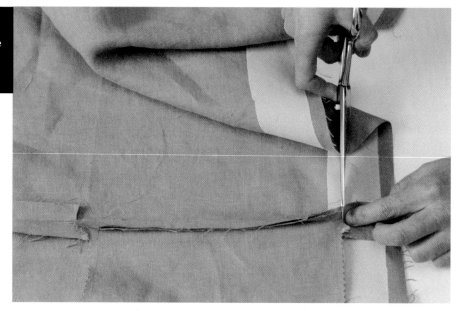

Release the pocket toward the front of the garment by clipping the back seam allowance above and below the pocket.

the pocket piece, then sew again from about 1½ in. above the bottom of the pocket piece to the hem of the garment. (The pocket needs to be deeper than the opening.) Baste across the pocket opening.

5. Press the side seams open. Clip the back seam allowances above and below the pocket, then press the pocket pieces toward the front of the garment (see the bottom photo above).

6. Pin, then baste the pocket pieces to the front of the garment. Using the basting stitches

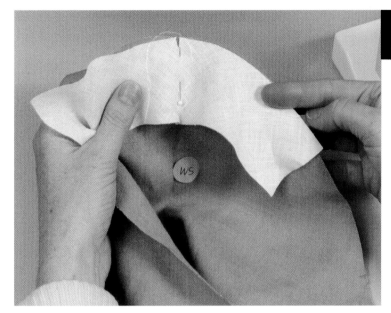

as a guide, topstitch the pocket piece in place from the right side.

7. Remove the basting stitches from the pocket opening and from the right side of the garment, then press.

Setting in sleeves

In the first part of this chapter, I introduced basic sleeve theory, whereby the sleeve cap is larger than the armscye because it encircles the arm, and then turns the corner at the top of the arm and fits over the shoulder. Sleeves are hard. It's important to take the time to check the sleeve/armscye lengths before you cut the fashion fabric and to take the time to ease and fit the sleeve into place. Here is how to set in a jacket sleeve.

1. Prepare the sleeve for setting in the garment by sewing the sleeve seams and finishing the seam allowances if the jacket will be unlined. If the pattern features a two-piece sleeve, sew both seams and finish them before setting the sleeve.

2. Cut a 2-in. by 8-in. strip of fabric from true bias (see p. 98). I recommend using linen or wool gabardine, but you could also use mohair, hair canvas, or lamb's wool, which is used by tailors. Fold the strip in half, and then make ⅛-in. snips at the center of both edges.

3. Place the strip on the wrong side of the sleeve, aligning the center snip of the strip to the tailor tack or mark that indicates the top of the sleeve. Then put the sleeve in the sewing machine, strip side up, and lower the needle into the fabric ⅜ in. from the raw edges at the center snip (see the top photo on p. 182).

4. Next, sew the strip to the top of the sleeve, pulling the bias strip as you go. The sewing machine won't want to move forward, so there will be a little fight going on between you and the machine. You don't want to win the fight

Sew from the center of the sleeve cap using a 3/8-in. seam allowance. Pull hard on the strip.

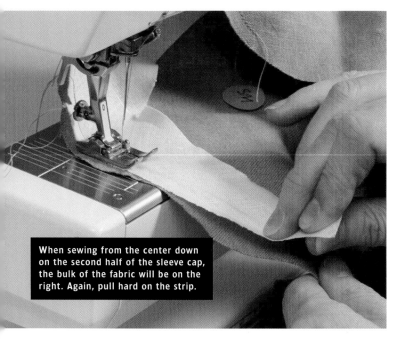

When sewing from the center down on the second half of the sleeve cap, the bulk of the fabric will be on the right. Again, pull hard on the strip.

completely, but you want the strip to be stretched as it is sewn to the sleeve.

5. Remove the sleeve from the machine. You'll notice that the sleeve is starting to take the shape you want it to have. The second side will be even harder to sew. Do this by turning the sleeve so that it is in the small side of the sewing machine and the strip is on the left. Repeat Steps 3 and 4.

6. Now, pin the sleeve to the armscye, matching the top of the sleeve to the shoulder, the bottom of the sleeve to the garment side seam, and the single front notch and the double back notches (see the photo at left on the facing page). Chances are the sleeve won't, but you will get an idea how much work you have left to do and where you have to do it.

7. If the sleeve is still too big for the armscye, unpin it and go back to the sewing machine. Staystitch-plus the sleeve, keeping your stitching within the 5/8-in. seam allowance. Continue until the fabric is crimped up enough to fit in the jacket. It's okay if you to ease all the way down the back of the sleeve to the underarm seam.

8. After you have eased the sleeve so that it matches the armscye, repin the sleeve in the garment and sew the armhole seam. I normally sew first with a longer stitch that is not quite a basting stitch. Check the seam for glitches. If there are a few places where a blip needs to be fixed, remove the stitches in that area, resew that part, and then sew the seam again. After fixing any glitches or if there aren't any, sew around this curved seam a second time with a regular stitch length.

9. Trim the seam allowance in the lower part of the sleeve from notch to notch, then press the seam allowances toward the sleeve.

Inserting shoulder pads

Most jackets look better with shoulder pads. I am not talking about how *you* look with

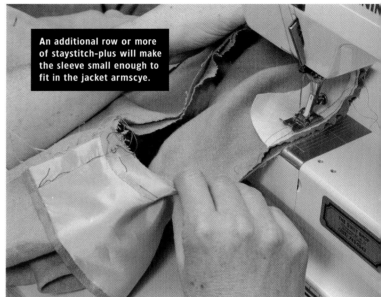

An additional row or more of staystitch-plus will make the sleeve small enough to fit in the jacket armscye.

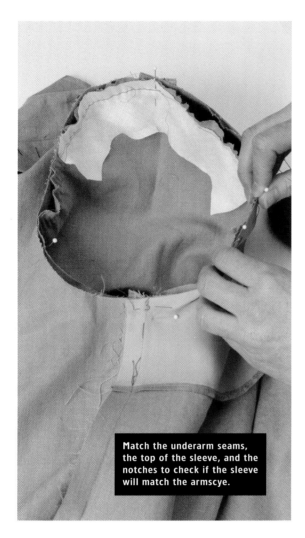

Match the underarm seams, the top of the sleeve, and the notches to check if the sleeve will match the armscye.

shoulder pads, just the jacket. A shoulder pad lifts the shoulder seam, evens out sloping shoulders, fills in gaps, and generally contributes to a good-looking jacket.

Collect a variety of shoulder-pad shapes to try on with different jacket styles. Some pads lift just at the edge (the epaulette style), some add a bit of shaping, and some are designed for use in drop-shoulder jackets.

If you choose shoulder pads that are constructed of polyester fibers, it will be necessary to cover the pad with fusible interfacing to keep it together during dry-cleaning. Here's how to cover a pad with interfacing and insert a shoulder pad.

1. Place each shoulder pad on a piece of fusible interfacing and cut out two pieces that are the shape of the pad plus about 1 in. all around (see the top photo on p. 184).

2. Position the interfacing on top of the pad, and then fold the pad in half. Keeping a press cloth between the iron and the pad, press, holding the iron in place for at least 10 seconds in each location (see the bottom left photo on p. 184). Unfold the shoulder pad.

3. Trim the interfacing to about ½ in. from the edge of the pad. Place a second piece of interfacing on the bottom of the pad and fuse in place, again taking care to use a press cloth so that the iron doesn't melt the interfacing and no resin sticks to the iron. Trim the bottom piece.

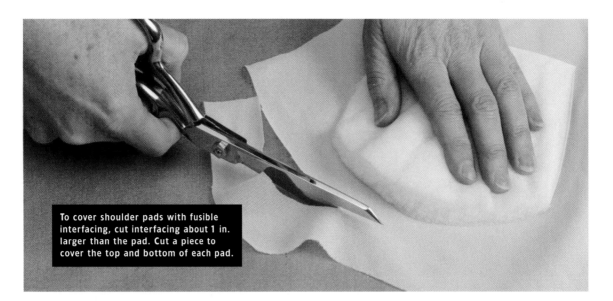

To cover shoulder pads with fusible interfacing, cut interfacing about 1 in. larger than the pad. Cut a piece to cover the top and bottom of each pad.

Place the interfacing on top of the pad, fold the pad in half, cover with a press cloth, and press, holding down the iron 10 seconds in each place until the piece is fused.

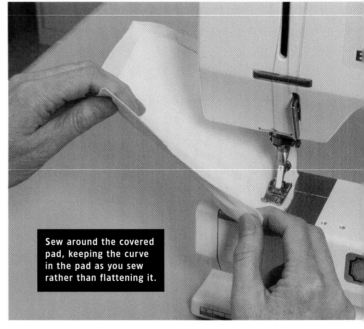

Sew around the covered pad, keeping the curve in the pad as you sew rather than flattening it.

4. Next, zigzag, overlock, or straight-stitch around the pad, keeping the pad curved as you sew. Trim close to the stitching.

An optional finish is to line the interfaced shoulder pad. To do this, cut pieces of lining fabric, then dart out excess fabric, if necessary, to get a good fit on the pad. Pin the lining to the underside of the pad, and then repin a piece on the top of the pad. Stitch close to the edge of the pad, then zigzag, overlock, or pink the edge of the lining fabric. You can add snaps to the pad and the shoulder seam for easy removal.

5. To attach the pad, fold it in half, then position it along the shoulder seam. Whipstitch the pad to each side of the shoulder seam. Don't stitch it down in the sleeve area (see the bottom photo at right).

Finishing the inside of the jacket

By shopping for ideas at my favorite stores, I've learned two ways to finish the inside of easy jackets that will prevent what I call "curling facing." Both of these techniques, fully facing and half-lining, are quicker than lining a jacket. I'll also give you a method of finishing the armhole seam allowances that will make the inside of your jacket look good.

FULLY FACING A JACKET Fully facing a jacket is one of the finishes I recommend for a great-looking, easy (but unlined) jacket. To fully face a jacket, it is necessary to cut two sets of jacket fronts—one that is actually the jacket front and one that replaces the jacket front facings. You will need approximately ¾ yd. of extra fabric.

1. Begin by interfacing the facing set of fronts, and then attach these fronts to the back neck facing.

2. Next, attach the full facing to the back neck facing.

3. Now attach the facing to the jacket along the next edge, sewing directionally from the center back of the neck edge all the way to the hems. To help this large piece stay in place, understitch the facing by sewing the seam allowances to the facing, stitching all three layers together as close as you can get to the seamline.

For a pretty finish, cover the pad again with lining fabric.

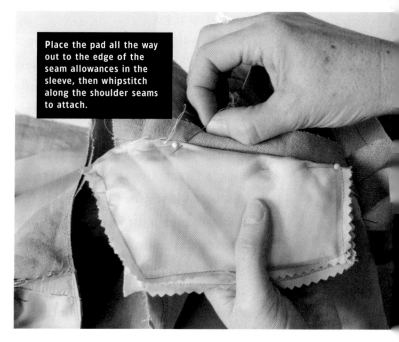

Place the pad all the way out to the edge of the seam allowances in the sleeve, then whipstitch along the shoulder seams to attach.

4. Press, then trim and grade the seams. Tailor-baste the neck and front edges of the garment all the way to the side seams.

5. Set the sleeves. Before trimming and finishing the sleeve seam allowances, sew the full facing to the sleeve seam allowances. Trim

FINISHING THE ARMHOLE SEAM ALLOWANCE—STEP 1

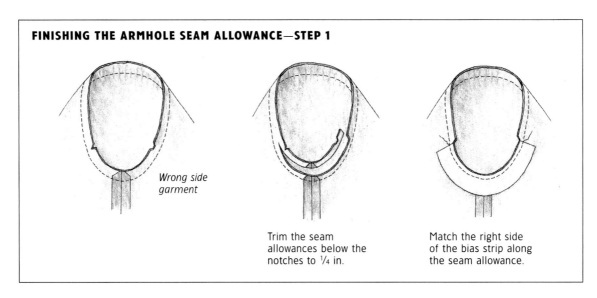

Wrong side garment

Trim the seam allowances below the notches to ¼ in.

Match the right side of the bias strip along the seam allowance.

FINISHING THE ARMHOLE SEAM ALLOWANCE—STEP 2

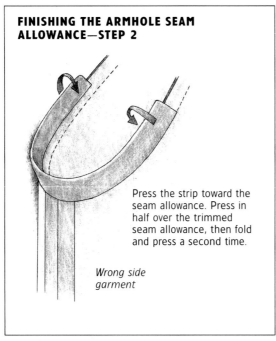

Press the strip toward the seam allowance. Press in half over the trimmed seam allowance, then fold and press a second time.

Wrong side garment

FINISHING THE ARMHOLE SEAM ALLOWANCE—STEP 3

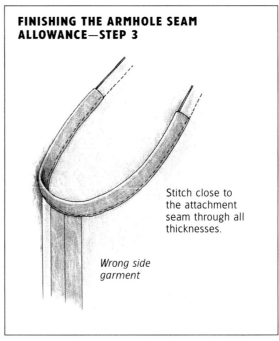

Stitch close to the attachment seam through all thicknesses.

Wrong side garment

SHIRT COLLARS Although some shirt collars are attached to jackets the hard way (as with a notched collar), I'm going to concentrate on the easy way to attach them.

1. Cut out and interface both the upper collar and the under collar. Trim ⅛ in. from the unnotched edges of the under collar. The notched edge is the neck edge, which you don't want to change.

2. Even though you have made the under collar smaller, match and pin the edges of the under collar to the edges of the upper collar. Sew the edges together, working with the upper collar on the bottom so that the sewing

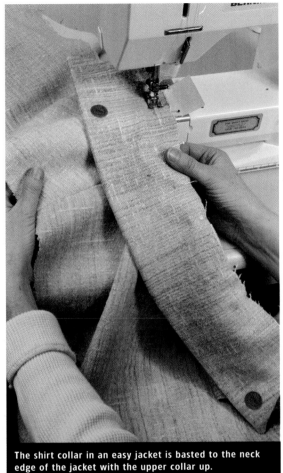

The shirt collar in an easy jacket is basted to the neck edge of the jacket with the upper collar up.

A mandarin collar is easy to add to a simple jacket before attaching the facings.

machine's feed dogs help you ease the two pieces together.

3. To get sharp corners, don't sew and pivot at the point. Instead, sew two or three stitches across the corner (typically best done by hand-turning the fly wheel so you have more control), then pivot and turn and sew toward the second collar point. Repeat at the other collar point.

4. Press the seam flat, and then, working on the edge of a tailor's pressing board, press the seams open. Trim, grading the seams so that the seam allowance closest to the upper collar is wider than the seam allowance closest to the under collar.

5. Next, baste the notched neck edges together, and baste the collar to the garment. The garment collar will be anchored in place when the back neck/front facings are attached.

MANDARIN COLLAR A mandarin collar is constructed similarly to an easy shirt collar.

1. Cut out and interface both the upper collar and the under collar. Trim ⅛ in. from the unnotched edges of the under collar. The notched edge is the neck edge, which you don't want to change.

2. Even though you have made the under collar smaller, match and pin the edges of the under collar to the edges of the upper collar. Sew the edges together, working with the upper collar on the bottom so that the sewing machine's feed dogs help you ease the two pieces together.

3. Press the seam flat, and then, working on the edge of a tailor's pressing board, press the seams open. Trim, grading the seams so that the seam allowance closest to the upper collar is wider than the seam allowance closest to the under collar.

4. Baste the notched neck edges together, and baste the collar to the garment, making sure that the upper collar is close to the garment since it will be flipped up when it is anchored in place by the back neck/front facings (see the photo below).

SHAWL COLLARS Shawl collar construction joins two differently shaped neck edges. To sew this collar successfully, you have to know how a square corner works.

1. Join the two collar pieces along the center back seam. Make sure you have marked the dots with tailor tacks or chalk marks.

2. Staystitch ½ in. on each side of the tailor tacks or chalk marks, pivoting at the dot. Remember that staystitching is stitching through a single layer of fabric, right next to

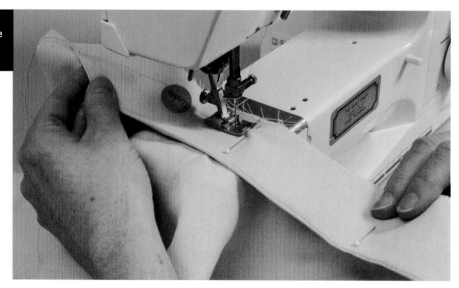

A mandarin collar is basted to the neck edge of the jacket with the under collar up.

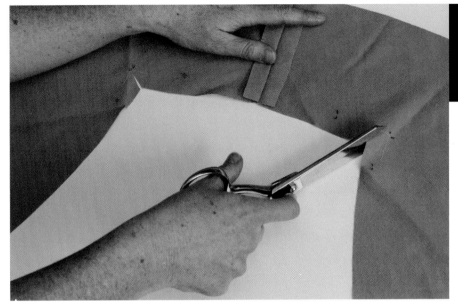

A shawl collar requires the construction of a square corner. Staystitch ½ in. on each side of the dots, and then clip to but not through each corner.

Sew exactly to the corner and put the needle down. Lift the presser foot and turn the garment, moving the excess fabric that was in front of the needle to the side and back. Sewing with the square corner side up lets you see what's going on.

the ⅝-in. seam allowance. Here's a place where I might use a smaller than normal stitch length.

3. Clip to the dot exactly (see the top photo above).

4. Next, staystitch the neck edge on the curved back neck facing. Fold the piece in half, and make a tiny snip in the center to give yourself an additional matchpoint.

5. With right sides together, match and pin the back neck facing to the collar along the neck edge. Match notches, dots, and center backs. To match the curved seam of the back neck facing to the collar, first match the corner

to the dot. Stick a pin straight down through the dot on the collar to the dot on the back neck facing. Pin here and pin the seam on one side of this corner. To sew, stitch to the dot, leave the needle down in the fabric, then lift the presser foot to turn, pin, and stitch the remainder of the seam (see the bottom photo on p. 191). Make sure when you start that the fabric is smooth and flat. After you lift the presser foot and turn the corner, move the excess fabric to the side you have finished sewing, making the area still to be sewn smooth and flat before lowering the presser foot and finishing the seam.

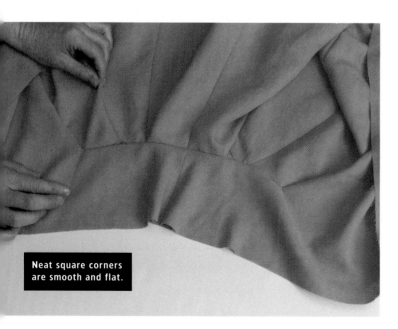

Neat square corners are smooth and flat.

■ STAGE IV: FINISHING

Unlike the garments made in the earlier chapters of this book, there is nothing fast and easy about making a jacket—at least not with me! Finishing a jacket is a time for celebration. The final steps in finishing your jacket include hemming and making buttonholes and attaching buttons.

Hemming the jacket

On a jacket, it is necessary to interface the sleeve hems and the jacket hem to prevent the hems from being wavy and crinkled. There are a couple of important things to remember. First, the interfacing has to be in the crease of the hem—not just on one side of the hem or the other.

Second, if you intend to line the jacket by machine, don't stitch the hem at the top; stitch about ⅝ in. below the top. The same goes for the sleeve hems.

To hem a jacket by hand, use a blindstitch or a blind catchstitch.

BLINDSTITCH Working right to left, take a small stitch in the hem, and then take a small stitch in the garment, catching only two or three threads on the garment side (see p. 74).

BLIND CATCHSTITCH Working left to right, take a small stitch in the hem. Then take a small stitch in the garment, catching only two or three threads and pulling the needle out over the thread on the needle. Come back to the hem and take another small stitch, pulling the needle out over the thread. Because you cross the thread each stitch, this is a good stitch for hemming (see p. 75).

Making buttonholes and attaching buttons

Once you make the buttonholes and attach the buttons, you can wear your jacket. This is incentive for attending to this task!

You may or may not have transferred the buttonhole markings to the jacket after you cut out the pattern. If you did, lay your buttons down on the jacket and see if the markings are still appropriate. If you did not, you have a bit more work to do.

1. To determine buttonhole size, measure the button you intend to use by wrapping a strip of paper around it. Pinch the paper sharply so you can see a mark, then slide the button out.

2. Flatten the paper and measure from the fold to the mark. This is the size buttonhole you need.

3. Always make a test buttonhole first. Do this by making a sandwich of two layers of fabric with interfacing to replicate the actual garment conditions. Make a buttonhole the size you determined in Step 2, and check to see that the button fits through it. Otherwise, adjust the size and make another sample.

4. Once you have determined the correct size buttonhole to make, mark the garment. Buttonholes on ladies' garments go on the right front. Leave a space that is at least half the diameter of the button plus $1/8$ in. between the edge of the garment and the start of the but-

tonhole. I make a line of basting stitches here, and mark the buttonholes from this line. I consider this the start line.

5. If the buttons are the same size as recommended by the pattern, keep the suggested spacing, otherwise play around with the buttons until you have the spacing the way you want it. Mark a horizontal line for each buttonhole, then mark each stop line.

6. Make the buttonholes. The best way to open up a buttonhole is with a buttonhole chisel. If you don't own this very sharp tool, place a pin at each end of the buttonhole. Starting in the center, use a sharp seam ripper to begin the cut, then work toward each pin with the seam ripper or with small, sharp scissors.

7. Attach the buttons using a needle threaded with double thread so that there are four threads on the needle. Knot the end of the thread.

Overlap and pin the garment fronts. Stick a pin through the buttonhole close to the center front edge of the garment, then slip the buttonhole over the pin. That's the mark for your button. When you sew the button, hold it up off the fabric. The double thread allows you to attach the button with only a couple of stitches. After the button feels secure, bring your needle up between the fabric and the button. Wrap the thread around the threads under the button, then bring the needle down to the wrong side of the garment to knot off.

Finished. Congratulations—now you're sewing!

making a kimono
in five easy lessons

■ ■ 6 ■

If you were to sign up for the beginning sewing class at The Sewing Workshop in San Francisco, you would be sent a kimono pattern in the mail with instructions for purchasing and preparing your fabric before you came to the first class. Our beginning class is five sessions, each three hours long. On the following pages, the sessions are separated into five days.

Pattern: Vogue 8155
Fabric: Cotton madras
Thread: Mettler silk-finish cotton
Needle: 70/10 H
Straight stitch, 2.5

Take the class with me now, by yourself or with a friend. We'll do everything together to make a simple kimono in five easy lessons and have a lot of fun along the way.

Before you start, make sure your sewing machine is in good working order. Put in a new needle and have an empty bobbin on hand. Find the manual that tells you how to thread the machine and the bobbin, or visit your sewing-machine dealer for a brush-up lesson.

■ DAY 1: GETTING STARTED

Before you can get going on your kimono, you'll need to take your measurements, select a pattern and fabric, and then prepare the fabric and cut out the pattern pieces. Set aside a block of time, and jump in!

Take basic measurements and buy a pattern

Our first session will take us to a fabric store, but you have to do a little homework first. You need to take a few basic measurements: your full bust, waist, and hip (see p. 17). Once you're at the fabric store, compare your measurements with the sizing chart on the pattern envelope. Purchase the pattern size based on this information.

Choose a style and determine how much fabric is needed

Look at the pattern envelope: Which style will you choose? The long robe or the short one? Look on the back of the pattern envelope and find the fabric chart. Find the size pattern you purchased and the style robe you intend to make. You will find that you have two choices of fabric width: 45 in. or 60 in. Highlight this part of the pattern envelope.

Choose and purchase fabric and notions

I recommend that you make your first garment in a natural-fiber fabric such as cotton, cotton flannel, stable (not loosely woven) rayon, or linen. If you think of the kimono as a beach cover-up, you might choose a light cotton with a great print; if you want something cozy, cotton flannel might be the choice for you. Avoid polyester and slippery, slinky fabrics for this project. If you choose a print, notice if the print is directional. If the fabric is striped, which way do the stripes run? If you fall in love with a fabric with stripes on the lengthwise grain, buy an extra ½ yd. of fabric. If the stripes are on the crosswise grain, you have too much work to do to make this an easy project. If you really love that fabric, buy

CONSTRUCTING
A KIMONO: DAY 1

- Take basic measurements.
- Buy a pattern.
- Choose a style.
- Determine how much fabric to buy.
- Choose and purchase fabric and notions.
- Prepare the fabric.
- Cut out the pattern pieces.
- Alter the pattern, if necessary.
- Read the pattern instructions.

½ yd. and make a pillow; buy something else for your kimono. Before you choose the fabric, review pp. 20-21 if you need to.

The salesperson will be able to tell you the fabric width, but you should also find that information on the end of the bolt along with the fabric fiber content and washing instructions. Purchase the amount of fabric you need and buy thread to match. Make sure you have scissors, pins, a tape measure, sewing needles, and contrasting thread on hand, or else buy them at the fabric store while you are there.

Prepare the fabric

When you get home from the fabric store, wash the fabric in the washing machine, and then put it in the dryer or hang it up to dry. If you need to, press the fabric after washing.

Cut out the pattern pieces

Take the pattern pieces out of the envelope and cut them apart. Cut off the black lines, which is a good habit to get into now, even though it won't matter on this oversized robe

tip *Get in the habit of starting on a project as soon as you bring the pattern and fabric home from the fabric store. If you prepare the fabric, cut out the pattern pieces, and read the pattern instructions, you are less likely to end up with a fabric stash and more likely to end up with finished garments.*

if you have an extra ⅛ in. here and there. If you are making a short kimono, find the front and back pattern pieces and the band piece. You'll need to cut off part of the paper pattern to make the short view, so look for the instruction on the pattern piece that says, "Cut off here for View A." Don't cut off at the lengthen/shorten lines—those lines are for alterations.

Alter the pattern if necessary

If you are tall, short, or have long arms, you may need to alter the pattern. Look on the back of the pattern envelope for the section listing finished lengths. To compare these measurements with your own, stand sideways in front of a mirror. If the robe you are making is 31½ in. long, find 31½ in. on your tape measure and put this at the nape of your neck—right where you can feel the top bone. The end of the tape measure is the length of the robe. Remembering that this is an oversized robe, I go with the "sort-ofs." Is "sort of" all right? If so, go with it. If you need to add less than 3 in., add it to the bottom. If you need to add more than 3 in., add half of it at the bottom and half between the lengthen/shorten lines on the pattern. To do this, cut the pattern apart between the lines and tape a piece of tissue paper there that equals the amount of length you need.

It's more difficult to decide if you need to add length for a kimono-style sleeve in a drop-shouldered garment. In this case, look at the line drawing and find the line that separates the sleeve from the garment front/back. It is below the shoulder in this pattern, so hold the pattern piece up to your arm about 3 in. below the shoulder.

If you want to add length, add a piece of tissue to the bottom of the sleeve, which is the end with no dot and no notches. If you want to add more than 3 in., add half of the length to the bottom of the sleeve and half along the lengthen/shorten lines on the pattern. Cut the pattern apart between the lines and tape a piece of tissue paper there that equals the amount of length you want.

Shortening is done the same way. Cut away some of the pattern from the bottom, unless you want to take away more than 3 in. In this case, take half of the amount from the bottom and half at the lengthen/shorten lines. By using the lengthen/shorten lines, you make the alteration proportional. Whether you are tall or short, this proportional altering is something you will do a lot.

Read the instructions

Take out the instruction sheet and read it over. There is a lot of information here. If you are confused about what information to pay attention to, review pp. 22-23. Most important, find the layout for the style you have chosen, the fabric width you have purchased, and the size you are making. Draw a circle around it.

This is a lot to do in one session, but you will be sewing before too long.

■ DAY 2: CUTTING AND MARKING

Today is the day you can really get going on your kimono. In this session, you will lay out and pin the pattern pieces, and then cut and mark the fabric.

Lay out and pin the pattern pieces

Take out your fabric and pattern pieces and the pattern's instruction sheet. You will need to work on a flat surface that is at least 1 yd. long, preferably longer. If you don't have a large table, folding cardboard cutting boards are available at most large fabric stores. Place the cutting board on top of a table or even on top of your bed.

With your pattern instructions as a guide, fold the fabric in half lengthwise, matching the selvage edges. This is a classic way to lay out a pattern. Pay attention to the abbreviations used for foldline (F/L) and selvage (S/L). Note the position of the selvages on the layout and turn the instruction sheet so that it matches the way your fabric is positioned.

If it's hard to get the selvages to meet, tug the fabric a bit. Sometimes washing and drying kinks up the fabric, but it's okay just to pull the

---

CONSTRUCTING
A KIMONO: DAY 2

- Lay out and pin the pattern pieces on the fabric.
- Cut out the garment pieces.
- Mark the garment pieces.

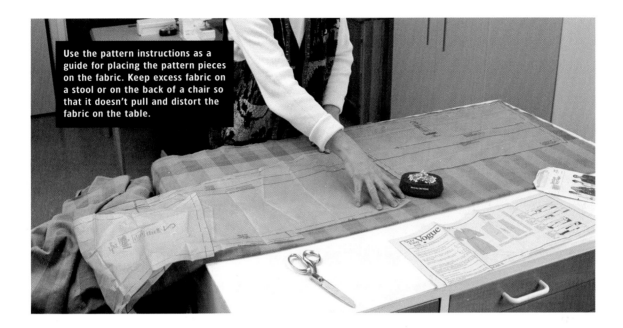

Use the pattern instructions as a guide for placing the pattern pieces on the fabric. Keep excess fabric on a stool or on the back of a chair so that it doesn't pull and distort the fabric on the table.

fabric on the diagonal so that the edges match. If the edges won't stay together, pin them about every 4 in. to 6 in. Fold and flatten, and pin the selvages if necessary, the entire length of fabric. Lay the fabric along the cutting surface with any excess fabric rolled up at one end or placed on the back of a chair or stool, so that the weight of the excess fabric doesn't distort the pattern layout.

Using your pattern instructions as a map, place each pattern piece on the fabric. Before pinning the entire pattern piece to the fabric, pin one end of the directional arrow. With a tape measure, measure the distance between the pinned line and the selvage edge, and then move to the other end of the arrow and measure from the selvage edge to the line (see the top photo on p. 200). Adjust the pattern piece so that it is equidistant from the selvage edge, then pin this end of the directional arrow. Pin

the rest of the pattern to the fabric, placing pins every 6 in. to 8 in., around the edge and and in every corner, smoothing the pattern out as you go. Make sure that the pins don't hang over the edge of the pattern.

Pin the rest of the pattern pieces in the same manner, measuring and pinning the directional arrows before pinning the pattern. This ensures that the pattern is on grain. If you have a directional print, go back and check that all

> **tip** *When a pattern piece is placed on the fold, it is not necessary to measure from the fold to the selvage edge to make sure the piece is straight. Because you have been careful folding the fabric, it is assumed that the selvage is parallel to the fold and already straight.*

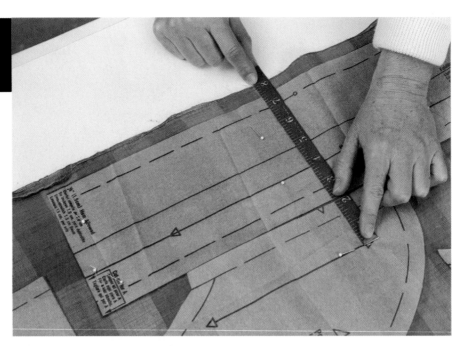

Keep the pattern piece parallel to the grain of the fabric by measuring from the arrow to the selvage at each end.

Pin and measure each piece.

the tops are at one end. Fold up the fabric with the pinned pieces as you go until all the pieces are pinned.

When laying out your pattern pieces, there are a few things to watch out for.

• Pattern pieces laid right side down are shaded on the instruction sheet.

• You are given only one pocket pattern piece, but notice that you are instructed to cut it twice. So pin the pocket piece but leave space to cut it again. After you have cut out all the pieces, go back and cut the pocket piece a second time.

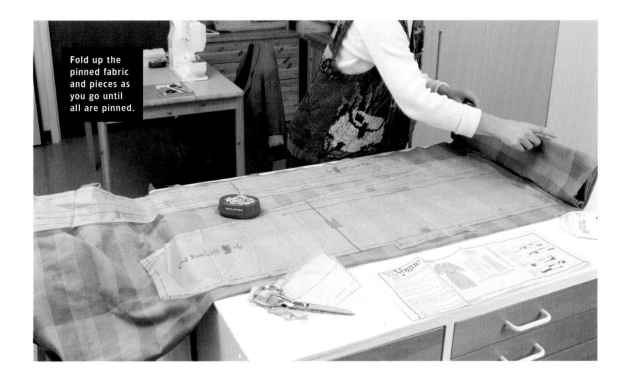

Fold up the pinned fabric and pieces as you go until all are pinned.

• Every now and then there will be a pattern piece you need only one of. The belt is one such piece. If you pinned the piece on folded fabric like all the other pattern pieces, you would end up with two belt pieces. Instead, by positioning this piece on the folded edge, matching the foldline on the pattern piece with the fold of the fabric, you will cut one belt piece that is folded in half. Note: Half the pattern piece is off the folded edge.

• If you are working with a directional print (see pp. 9–10), all the tops of the pieces have to be at one end of the fabric. For the most part, the pattern instructions have done this, but watch out for the band since it's hard to tell which end is the top. Hint: The top of that piece is the notched edge. According to the pattern instructions, the sleeve is positioned along the lengthwise grain.

With a directional print, this piece is better positioned along the crosswise grain. See if there is enough fabric and if it is wide enough to cut two pieces along the crosswise grain, and do this if possible. Otherwise, the print will go around the sleeve, rather than up and down.

Cut out the garment pieces

It sounds so simple to say, "Cut out the garment pieces." Away you go, but with a few hints. First, don't lift and hold the fabric with one hand and cut with the other. Rather, place one hand flat on the fabric and cut with the other (see the top photo on p. 202). Second, don't take short cuts; use the full length of the scissor blade. Third, keep the scissors straight, not tilted one way or the other. Fourth, cut out each piece along the edge of the pattern. When you are finished cutting, remember to pin and

Keep the fabric flat as you cut, and use the full length of the scissors—no short, choppy cuts.

Tailor-tack the dots.

cut a second set of pocket pieces before tossing away your scraps. Last, save a couple of scraps for practicing on the sewing machine and for belt loops.

Mark the garment pieces

Your next task is to mark the garment pieces. The markings on this garment are notches and a few dots. For each notch found along the edge of the pattern, make a ⅛-in. snip—don't cut a V in the fabric or make giant snips. The snips are matchpoints, so it isn't necessary or wise to cut too far into the seam allowance or to cut too much of it away.

For the dots, you have a couple of options. In my beginning sewing classes, I teach students to make tailor tacks using a thread that contrasts in color to the garment fabric. To make tailor tacks, thread a needle with a double thread and double the thread so that there are four threads on the needle. Don't knot the thread. Wherever you find a dot—either a large dot or a small one—take a stitch through all layers of pattern and fabric. Just go down through all the layers and come back up to the side you started from. Leave a 1-in. thread tail on each side of the stitch, and cut the thread.

Next, carefully separate the fabric layers so you can see the threads, and then cut them. You have made a mark on each side of each piece of fabric, and because you have used four threads, the marks tend to stay in place longer.

This is an old-fashioned way of marking. You can mark with any number of devices such as chalk, chalk pencils, or fabric marking pens.

■ DAY 3: TIME TO SEW!

The fun part of sewing is sitting down at the machine and putting together the pieces. It doesn't take too much practice at the machine before you are ready to sew the garment.

Thread the machine

Open the sewing machine manual to the page that tells you how to wind the bobbin, since we are going to do that first. Thread the bobbin casing and then thread the machine. Next practice sewing on some of the scraps.

Practice sewing straight

When sewing two pieces of fabric together, pin each end and about every 5 in. between. I place the pins parallel to the seam, pointed in

---

CONSTRUCTING
A KIMONO: DAY 3

- Thread the machine.
- Practice sewing straight.
- Practice simple seam finishes.
- Sew the first seam.
- Add the fronts.

Pin the pieces right sides together. If you can't tell the right side of the fabric from the wrong side, mark the fabric using chalk or peel-and-stick labels.

the direction I am going to sew, but you can also pin horizontally. Just remember that you have to take the pins out as you go. You don't want to sew over the pins—it's not good for the pins, for the needle, or for the machine.

For a seam guide, I place a Post-It self-stick note along the ⅝-in. line to the right of the needle so that I have a clearly visible line to place the edges of my fabric along. To sew, bring the pinned edge of the fabric right under the needle. Put the presser foot down, turn the fly wheel so that the needle goes into the fabric, then put a finger on the thread tail so you don't get a big wad of thread under the fabric when you start to sew. Take the first pin out and begin sewing, keeping an even pressure on the foot pedal.

Starting at the edge of the fabric, sew a few stitches, then backstitch a few stitches (make sure it's only a few stitches—you don't need ½ in. of backstitching). Continue sewing all the way to the other edge, taking the pins out as you sew, and then backstitch a few stitches. Don't sew off the end; stop when you get there.

Start sewing at the edge of the fabric, sew a few stitches, and then backstitch one or two stitches to lock them.

Practice sewing a few straight lines, then using two pieces of fabric, sew a couple of seams. Press the seams, too. To press a seam, first press the seam just the way it is. Next, press the seam open on the wrong side of the fabric, and then press the seam from the right side of the fabric.

Practice simple seam finishes

Once you start putting the garment pieces together, you get to make your first decision: What do you want the garment to look like on the inside? Sewing teachers love this technical stuff, but you can actually have a good-looking robe using a not-so-difficult seam finish. The pattern instructions tell you which pieces to

> **tip** *Various guides for sewing straight include devices that attach to the sewing machine with a magnet, screw, or tape. I prefer the low-tech Post-It or even a rubber band. These don't leave marks or tape residue or, like a magnet, interfere with the machine's electronics.*

sew together but not the options you have for finishing the seams.

STITCH AND PINK An easy way to finish a seam is to stitch and pink.

1. After completing the seam and pressing it open, sew a line of stitches along each side of the seam allowance. It is important to sew through one layer of fabric only. Line up the sewing machine presser foot with the seamline to help keep your stitches straight.

2. After sewing, cut the edge of the seam allowance with pinking shears.

MOCK-FELL SEAMS Another seam finish to consider is a mock-fell seam. This seam finish also contains raveling but takes less time (and a little less skill) to construct than classic flat-fell seams. Construct a mock-fell seam as follows:

1. After sewing and pressing the seams, trim one side of the seam allowance to ⅜ in. Pink or overlock the untrimmed seam allowance or leave it unfinished.

2. Press the untrimmed seam allowance flat over the trimmed one and pin or pin and baste onto the garment.

3. Sew the untrimmed seam allowance down, keeping the stitching line parallel to the seamline. The trimmed seam allowance will be hidden by the stitched-down seam allowance. (Because it is easy to keep your stitches parallel to the seamline, it is not necessary to sew from the right side of the garment.)

FLAT-FELL SEAM A third method of finishing a seam is to sew a flat-fell seam, which is constructed as follows:

1. After sewing and pressing the seam allowance, trim one side of the seam allowance

by ⅜ in. Press the untrimmed seam allowance over the trimmed one, then press it in half, tucking the trimmed seam allowance inside. Pin or pin and baste the folded seam allowance along the folded edge.

2. Turn the garment right side up. From the right side of the garment, topstitch the folded seam allowance in place in line with the folded edge, following the basting line or the line of pins. The stitching line should be parallel to the seams.

Sew the first seam

After you've practiced, it's time to sew the first seam following the pattern instructions. Start with pattern piece No. 1, the back. Remove the paper pattern piece from the garment pieces. Determine which is the right side of the fabric and which is the wrong, then mark the wrong side with peel-and-stick labels or chalk. Place the fabric pieces right sides together.

Before you pin, remember that you have a small opening on the right side of the sewing machine needle and a space as big as your table on the left side. You want to pin the fabric so that the big part is on the left and the little seam allowance is on the right.

Pin the center back seam of piece No. 1, first at each end and then where the notches are. (There are three notches in the center back, which is a standard marking.) Pin the rest of the seam at about 5-in. intervals. This is the longest seam you will have to sew in the whole garment, and it's nice to get it out of the way first.

As you sew keep the pinned edges of the fabric along the edge of the Post-It note. Re-

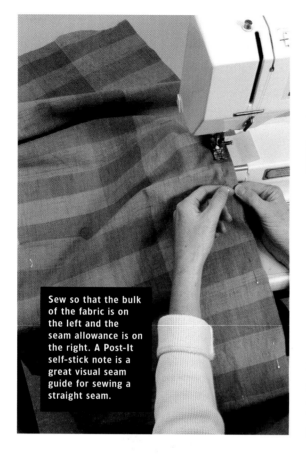

Sew so that the bulk of the fabric is on the left and the seam allowance is on the right. A Post-It self-stick note is a great visual seam guide for sewing a straight seam.

> **tip** *Say this to yourself over and over: Right sides together, right sides together, right sides together. Most sewing is done right sides together, and repeating this phrase will help you remember.*

member to backstitch at the beginning and end of the line of stitches. Press the seam flat and then open. Then finish the seam.

Add the fronts

"Sew back to front at shoulder seams" is the second step in sewing this kimono. To do this, place the back piece right side up on a flat surface. Place each front piece right side down, lining up the shoulder seams only. It doesn't matter if any of the other edges match.

Press the seam flat, then open.

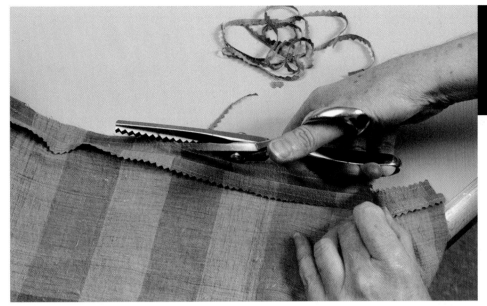

Stitch along the center of each seam allowance, and then pink the edges. This seam finish prevents raveling and the seams look neat.

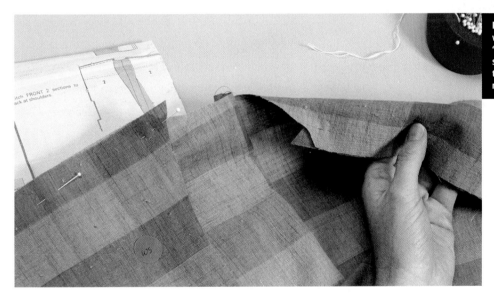

Remember that when you sew "back to front at shoulder seams" the edges don't match.

Look closely at the shoulder seams. The front piece curves in toward the neck and the back pieces curve straight up. This is nothing to worry about. These pieces match ⅝ in. from the edge where the seam is, so this is what is important. Pin and sew the shoulder seams, then press and finish them.

■ DAY 4: MAKING PROGRESS

Today is a sewing day. Put on a favorite CD, and enjoy the sewing process. Refer to the pattern instructions regularly. Although I will be adding bits of information to the instructions, we are basically following the step-by-step guide provided.

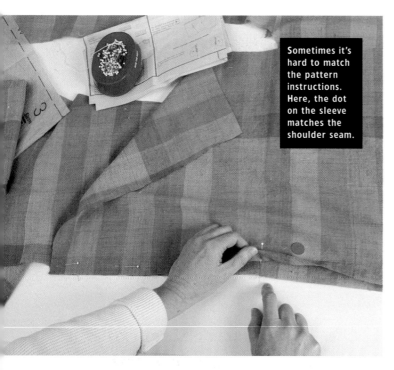

Sometimes it's hard to match the pattern instructions. Here, the dot on the sleeve matches the shoulder seam.

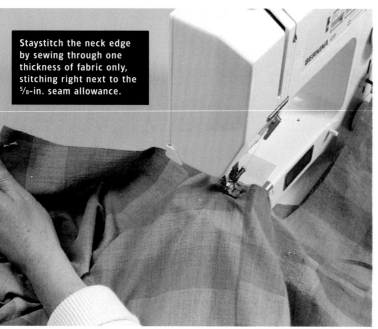

Staystitch the neck edge by sewing through one thickness of fabric only, stitching right next to the 5/8-in. seam allowance.

Attach the sleeves

In general, my advice to people who are new to deciphering pattern instructions is to make your garment look like the picture in the

- Attach the sleeves.
- Staystitch the neck edge.
- Attach the pockets.
- Sew the back to the front along the side seams.

instructions. In this pattern, however, it's hard to decipher the picture for attaching this sleeve, which illustrates only part of the robe and is viewed from the wrong side. Let me translate for you, so you will know how to attach the sleeves.

Place the kimono pieces that you have sewn together on a flat surface, right side up, so you can see the whole garment. Next, take the paper pattern piece off pattern piece No. 3, which is the sleeve. Note that each sleeve piece has a dot that will match along the edge of the kimono back and one notch that will match along the edge of the kimono front.

Place each sleeve piece right side down so that the sleeve partly covers the robe. With the marked edge (the one with the dot and the notches) along the side edge of the kimono, pin each sleeve in place, matching the dot to the shoulder seam, the two notches on the sleeve to the two notches on the robe, and the single notch on the sleeve to the single notch on the robe. The sleeves will overlap when pinned, but they will flip into place after you have sewn the seam. Sew, press, then finish the seams.

Sew the underarm seam as a square corner, then reinforce the corner by sewing it again, ½ in. on each side of the corner.

Curved edges of pockets point to the hem edges. Match and pin the pocket pieces to the pocket extensions ⅝ in. from the edge.

Staystitch the neck edge

The next thing the pattern instructions tell you to do is to staystitch the neck edge. Staystitching is sewing through one layer of fabric; it is used to stabilize edges such as the neckline. Using a regular-length stitch, sew from dot to dot around the neck edges of the kimono.

Attach the pockets

With right sides together, position each pocket piece on each pocket extension, positioning the curved end of the piece toward the hem. Pin and sew all four seams. This is a great way to get a lot of sewing done fast. Press the pockets out, away from the garment, and finish each of these short seams.

Sew the back to the front along the side seams

The sleeves, side seams, and pockets are all finished next. Fold the kimono right sides together, lining up the edges of the sleeves, the side seams, the pocket bags, and the hems. As the instructions indicate, sew along the sleeve, turn the corner at the side seam, and sew to the first dot that marks the pocket opening. Then sew from the second dot to the hem.

When you sew the corner, make it square. Do this by sewing along the sleeve seam to the side seam. Leave the needle in the fabric, lift the presser foot, turn the fabric, and continue sewing. I suggest making small reinforcing stitches in the corner since you will have to clip here. To reinforce, go back and stitch on top of the previous stitching about ½ in. on each side of the corner (see the right photo above).

Clip to the corner, making sure you cut to but not through the stitches.

Once the side seam is finished, sew around the pocket bag. At the top of the pocket, start at the seamline, sewing ⅝ in. away from the edge of the pocket. At the bottom of the pocket, sew all the way to the dot—don't leave any holes.

When you have completed sewing the sleeve, side seams, and pockets, clip to the corner at the square corner, above the pocket, and below the pocket. The magic words are "to but not through" the stitching line, meaning right

tip *How will you know when and how to change a pattern? By trial and error. First, keep your seam ripper handy, take out what doesn't look good, and try again. Second, ask someone you know who sews. Third, consult the most knowledgeable salesclerk at your favorite fabric store.*

tip *Without clipping, the underarm seam would be badly puckered on the outside. Clipping releases the two sides of the corner so each can go in the direction it wants to go. If you find yourself saying, "What did I do wrong here?" maybe you just forgot to clip the corner.*

up to the stitching line, not even ⅛ in. away. Now you can finish these side seams in three sections.

We are moving along to pattern piece No. 5, the band. This robe is almost finished! Take the paper pattern pieces off the band and seam the notched edges together. This is one seam you don't have to finish. Before you stop for the day, press ⅝ in. of the long, unnotched edge to the wrong side. The pattern says to baste and trim, but because you are using a natural-fiber fabric, you will be okay if you just press.

■ DAY 5: LET'S FINISH THIS PROJECT!

The first thing to do today is to hem the bottom of the robe and the sleeves. The bottom hem, in particular, needs to be done before the

CONSTRUCTING A KIMONO: DAY 5

- Hem the garment and the sleeves.
- Attach the band.
- Make the belt.
- Make the belt loops.

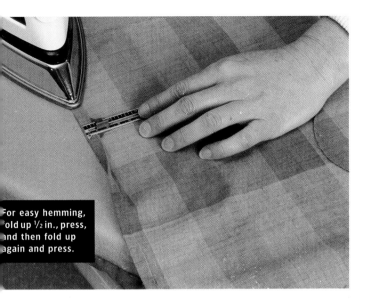

For easy hemming, fold up ½ in., press, and then fold up again and press.

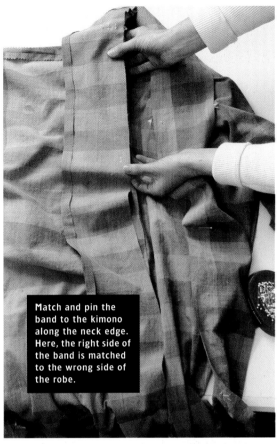

Match and pin the band to the kimono along the neck edge. Here, the right side of the band is matched to the wrong side of the robe.

band is attached and the garment needs to be shorter than the band is long.

Hem the garment and the sleeves

Try on the garment to check the length. This is an easy garment, so we are going to make an easy hem: stitching it in place on the sewing machine. The pattern instructions tell you to fold up ⅝ in., and then to fold under ¼ in. My translation is to turn up ¼ in. and press, then turn up ½ in. and press. This is a bit more than the pattern allows, but remember that this is an oversize robe and it doesn't really have to have a ⅝-in. hem. Hem the sleeves the same way: Fold up ½ in., press, turn up ½ in., and press again. Topstitch.

Attach the band

All of the sewing so far has been right sides together, which is almost always the case. Except now. To attach the band, place the right side of the band against the wrong side of the robe, matching the unpressed edge of the band with the front edge of the robe. Start by matching the seam on the band with the center back seam on the robe. Pin, matching the dots and notches on the band to the dots and notches on the robe (see the photo above).

Sew, then press the band and the seam allowances away from the robe.

Here comes the tricky part. Fold the band in half with *right sides together*. Don't let the band overlap the robe at all. Do this at both ends of the band. You are going to sew a line from the bottom of the hem across the folded band. If you want, draw the sewing line with chalk or use a line of pins to help you sew straight.

When sewing, don't catch the hem in this seam; make sure it is separate.

Trim the seam allowance, and flip the band right side out. By the magic of following instructions, you have created a very professional-looking finished band. Now to finish it.

Press the band in half with *wrong sides together,* and line up the pressed-under seam allowance along the front edge of the robe. Pin, matching the dots. This step is very important. Use lots of pins. Take care that the edges match along the neckline edge, which is slightly curved.

The next step is to topstitch the band in place. When doing this, it is important that you don't let one layer of fabric creep ahead of the other, which can sometimes happen when you are sewing long pieces of fabric together. To prevent creeping, hold the band behind and in front of the needle with some tautness while sewing. Don't stretch or pull—just hold the fabric taut (see the photo at right below).

The bottom of the band is finished by folding it in half with right sides together, then sewing across in line with the hem. Trim the edge, then flip it right side out.

To keep the band from shifting as you topstitch it, pin all matchpoints and hold the fabric taut in front and in back of the needle.

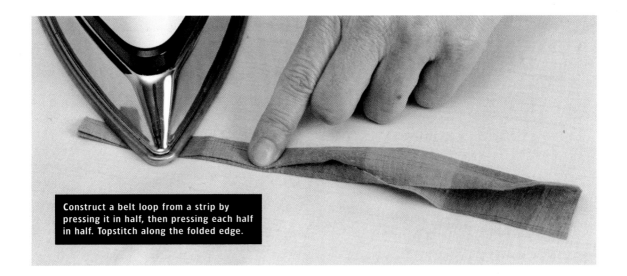

Construct a belt loop from a strip by pressing it in half, then pressing each half in half. Topstitch along the folded edge.

Aren't you proud of yourself? You've just made a kimono!

Make the belt

Making the belt is easy. With right sides together, fold and pin the belt in half. Sew across one short end, turn the corner, and sew toward the center, stopping about 5 in. from the center. Sew across the second short end, turn the corner, and sew toward the center, again stopping about 5 in. from the center.

Trim the corners, then push each end in toward the center to turn the belt right side out through the unsewn part in the center. Press the belt. Finish by machine-stitching along the opening or by slipstitching the opening closed.

Make the belt loops

If you want to add belt loops, cut a scrap piece of fabric so that it is an even rectangle, about 8 in. long and 1½ in. to 2 in. wide. On the ironing board, fold the piece in half, then fold each half in half (see the photo above). Topstitch the folded edges together, then cut the piece into two 4-in. pieces.

On each side seam, determine where you need a belt loop. Place it above the pocket but close to it because you need to blouse up the robe some. Fold and pin the unfinished edges under. If your fabric is thick, such as cotton flannel, you should change the sewing machine needle to a larger size so that you can sew through all the thicknesses. Sew a square or an X at each end to attach the belt loop.

Now, of course, you need to send me a picture of your finished project, preferably with you wearing it! This is actually a long project for a first one. For your next garment, make something simple, like the vest in Chapter 3 (that's only a three-class garment).

Happy sewing!

resources

Sewing Supplies

Clotilde
B3000
Louisiana, MO 63353-3000
(800) 772-2891

Nancy's Notions
P.O. Box 683
Beaverdam, WI 53916
(800) 833-0690

The Sewing Workshop
2010 Balboa St.
San Francisco, CA 94121
(800) 466-1599

Fabrics by Mail

Banksville Designer Fabrics
115 New Canaan Ave.
Norwalk, CT 06850
(203) 846-1333

Britex Fabrics
146 Geary St.
San Francisco, CA 94108
(415) 392-2910

G Street Fabrics
Mail Order Services
12240 Wilkins Ave.
Rockville, MD 20852
(800) 333-9191

Threadwear
1250 S.W. Oakley Ave.
Topeka, KS 66604
(800) 466-1599

index

Note: Italics indicate a photograph or illustration.